Abitur*Skript*

Englisch

Gymnasium · Gesamtschule

STARK

Inhalt

UK – between tradition and change

1	**The UK's geography**	1
1.1	Countries of the United Kingdom	2
1.2	The English north-south divide	2
2	**The UK's history**	3
2.1	Scotland and the issue of devolution	5
2.2	From Empire to Commonwealth	7
3	**The UK's politics**	9
3.1	The UK's political parties	10
3.2	British monarchy	11
3.3	The UK and the EU (Brexit)	13
4	**UK society**	15
4.1	British (multicultural) identity	15
4.2	Class system in the UK	17
4.3	Religion	19
5	**UK culture**	20

USA – between tradition and change

1	**The USA's geography**	21
2	**The USA's history**	22
2.1	The USA's foreign policy: From isolationism to becoming "the policeman of the world"	25
2.2	The terrorist attacks of 9/11	27
3	**The USA's politics**	28
3.1	Checks and balances in US politics	28
3.2	The Democratic Party and the Republican Party	30
4	**USA society**	31
4.1	The USA as an "immigrant country"	31
4.2	The American Dream and other central concepts of American identity	34
4.3	The USA and violence	36
4.4	Religion	39

5   USA culture 41

Global chances and challenges

1   Globalisation and the economy 44

2   Globalisation and the environment 47

3   Globalisation and culture 49

4   Globalisation and politics 51

The media

1   History of the media 53

2   Traditional media 54

3   Media literacy 55

4   The digital age 56

Science and technology

1   **Biotechnology and genetic engineering** 59

1.1   Green biotechnology 60

1.2   Red biotechnology 61

1.3   White biotechnology 63

2   **Artificial intelligence (AI)** 63

3   **Future worlds in literature** 65

3.1   Utopia – dystopia 65

3.2   Science fiction 68

The English-speaking world – between tradition and change

1   **Ireland** 69

1.1   Country profile 69

1.2   History 70

1.3   Ireland today and in the future 71

2   **India** 73

2.1   Country profile 73

2.2   History 74

2.3	India today and in the future	75
3	**South Africa**	77
3.1	Country profile	77
3.2	History	78
3.3	South Africa today and in the future	79
4	**Nigeria**	81
4.1	Country profile	81
4.2	History	82
4.3	Nigeria today and in the future	83

Shakespeare and his time

1	**Biography and historical background**	86
1.1	Historical overview	86
1.2	The Elizabethan worldview	87
1.3	Life and inspirations	88
1.4	Theatre in Shakespeare's time	88
2	**Works**	89
2.1	Comedies	89
2.2	Tragedies	90
2.3	Histories	91
2.4	Sonnets	91
3	**Language**	92
4	**Shakespeare – still relevant today?**	93

Stichwortverzeichnis

Autor: Dr. Dirk Großklaus

Vorwort

Liebe Schülerinnen und Schüler,

dieses handliche Skript widmet sich den für Ihr **Englisch-Abitur** wesentlichen Inhalten. Je nachdem, ob Sie in Englisch mündlich oder schriftlich geprüft werden, werden unterschiedliche Inhalte Gegenstand Ihrer Prüfung sein.

Für die **mündliche Prüfung** setzen Sie in Absprache mit Ihrer Lehrkraft **eigene Schwerpunkte**. Sie können also selbst entscheiden, welche Kapitel Sie für Ihre Vorbereitung brauchen.

Für die **schriftliche Prüfung** sind die relevanten Themengebiete normalerweise vorgegeben. Über nebenstehenden QR-Code gelangen Sie zu einer Übersicht, die Ihnen zeigt, welche Kapitel für die Prüfung in Ihrem Bundesland besonders relevant sind.

https://www.stark-verlag.de/
10546S/uebersicht

In seiner klaren Struktur und Fokussierung eignet sich das Skript hervorragend zur Auffrischung und Wiederholung des Prüfungsstoffs kurz vor dem Abitur. Folgende Elemente helfen Ihnen dabei, es optimal zu nutzen:

- Wichtige Begriffe sind **fett** hervorgehoben.

- Mit Rauten markierte Kästen erklären wichtige **Fachausdrücke** und definieren zentrale Aspekte eines Themas.

- Zahlreiche **Schaubilder**, **Grafiken** und **Tabellen** fassen die Inhalte übersichtlich zusammen und erleichtern so das Lernen.

- discussion topic Zu allen Diskussionsthemen gibt es mit Ausrufezeichen gekennzeichnete **Listen mit wichtigen Argumenten**. Diese helfen vor allem bei der Vorbereitung auf mündliche Prüfungen oder freie Schreibaufgaben.

Viel Erfolg beim Lernen mit diesem Buch und im Abitur!

Dr. Dirk Großklaus

UK – between tradition and change

1   The UK's geography

- **The United Kingdom of Great Britain and Northern Ireland:** often simply referred to as the "United Kingdom", the "UK" or "Britain"; politically, a unitary state
- **Great Britain:** the largest of the British Isles, comprising England, Wales and Scotland
- **British Isles:** geographical term meaning the group of islands in the north-west of continental Europe, including Great Britain, Ireland and smaller islands

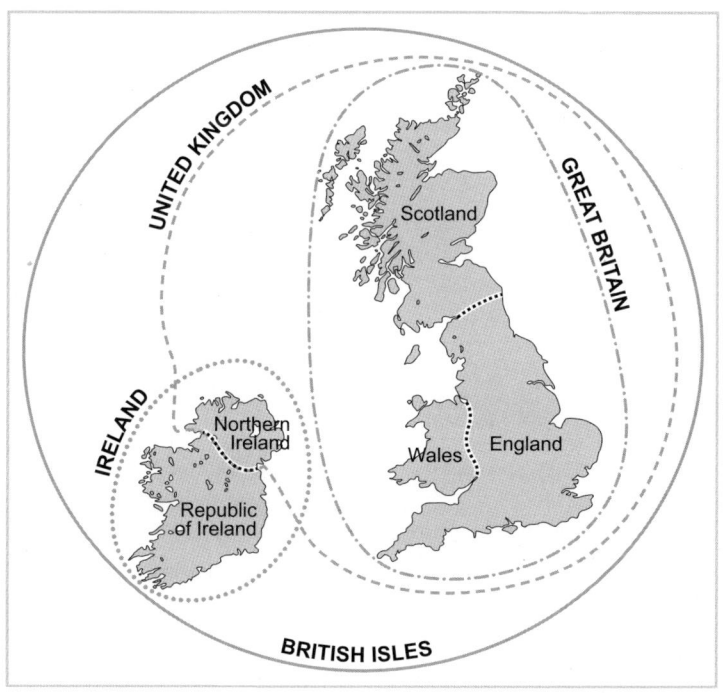

1.1 Countries of the United Kingdom

- The United Kingdom is a **unitary sovereign state** made up of four different countries: England, Wales, Scotland and Northern Ireland.

- During a process of **devolution**, Scotland, Wales and Northern Ireland acquired a form of autonomy, at least in some areas.

- **England**, as the largest and most populous country in the UK, is also the only one without a local government.

- Due to a pronounced **north-south divide** in England, there are often cries for a new devolution, from which the "Northerners" could profit as they currently often feel underrepresented and underfunded.

Overview of the UK's four countries

	Country	Capital	Size	Population	Devolved legislative body
	England	London	~ 130,000 km²	~ 55 m	none (but: London Assembly)
	Scotland	Edinburgh	~ 78,000 km²	~ 5.4 m	Scottish Parliament
	Wales	Cardiff	~ 21,000 km²	~ 3.1 m	Senedd (Welsh Parliament)
	Northern Ireland	Belfast	~ 14,000 km²	~ 1.9 m	Northern Ireland Assembly

1.2 The English north-south divide

	The north	The south
Economy	mainly public sector	also private investments
Income	lower	higher
Unemployment	higher	lower
House prices	lower	higher

Education	on average lower marks, less opportunity for students to study at elite universities	more top marks, best schools and universities concentrated in the south
Life expectancy	lower	higher

2 The UK's history[1]

Important stages in British history	
43 – ~410	large parts of Great Britain under **Roman occupation** (Celtic resistance)
from 5th century onwards	**Angles**, **Saxons** and **Jutes** invade the British Isles and establish several kingdoms
~8th to 11th centuries	continued **Viking attacks** and settlement on British land
1066	**Norman Conquest:** William the Conqueror defeats the last Saxon King Harold in the Battle of Hastings
1215	**Magna Carta:** agreement between King John and the barons to grant the latter more rights; mythicised as the first "democratic" document
1455 – 1485	**Wars of the Roses:** fought between the House of Lancaster (symbol: red rose) and the House of York (symbol: white rose); Henry VII founds a new dynasty, the Tudors
1534	**English Reformation:** Henry VIII separates the Church of England from Rome and the monarch becomes the head of the Church
1558 – 1603	**Elizabethan Age:** Elizabeth I's reign, England becomes Europe's leading sea power, foundation of the British Empire, time of flourishing sciences and arts (e. g. Shakespeare)
1642 – 1651	**English Civil War** between the Crown and Parliament troops

1 To focus on Scottish history, see "Scotland and the issue of devolution" (pp. 5/6), for (Northern) Irish history, see chapter on Ireland in "The English-speaking world" (pp. 69 – 72).

Important stages in British history	
1649–1660	11 years as a **republic** (with Oliver Cromwell as "Lord Protector" from 1653 to 1658)
1688/1689	the **"Glorious Revolution"** (Bill of Rights, 1689) strengthens Parliament's position and makes Britain a constitutional monarchy
18th century	Britain becomes **the world's leading colonial power** (despite the loss of the Thirteen American Colonies in 1783)
~1760–1840	**Industrial Revolution:** change from a society that was agricultural and based on cottage industry to one that was industrialised and factory-based (British head start, Britain as "the workshop of the world")
1837–1901	**Victorian Age:** Queen Victoria's reign, height of the British Empire, groundbreaking progress in science and technology
1914–1918	**World War I**
1918	**suffrage** for all men (without property restrictions) over 21 and some women (with property restrictions) over 30
1928	**equal suffrage** for women and men over 21 (without property restrictions)
1939–1945	**World War II**
1945	Britain is one of the founding members of the **United Nations**
second half of the 20th century	continued **decline of the British Empire** (the handing over of Hong Kong to China in 1997 is seen as the official end of the British Empire)
1953	coronation of Queen Elizabeth II
1973	Britain joins the **EC** (European Communities, later to become the **EU**)
1979–1990	Margaret Thatcher's time as Prime Minister: **"Thatcherism"** is a time of reduced social spending and decisive action against trade unions
2003	beginning of **Iraq War**
2012	London Olympics

Important stages in British history	
2016	**Brexit referendum:** 51.9 % of the British vote to leave the EU
2020	Britain officially **leaves the EU**
2022	Queen Elizabeth II dies after a reign of 70 years

2.1 Scotland and the issue of devolution

- **devolution:** different from **federalism** because in a federal system the states' powers are **constitutionally fixed** whereas in devolution a **central government decides** to grant more powers to its substates
- **Holyrood:** area in the Scottish capital Edinburgh where the Scottish Parliament is located (the term "Holyrood" is also used as a synonym for "Scottish Parliament")
- **First Minister:** leader of the Scottish (or another devolved) government

Important stages in Scottish history	
1603	**Union of the Crowns:** Elizabeth I dies childless. James VI of Scotland also becomes James I of England (Stuart dynasty), but there are still two separate parliaments.
1707	**Treaty of Union:** new United Kingdom with a single parliament
1746	**Battle of Culloden:** serious defeat of Scottish Highlanders (under "Bonnie Prince Charlie", who claims a right to the British throne) → Battle of Culloden as a typical example of English oppression in Scottish national consciousness
1934	The **Scottish National Party (SNP)** is established. It campaigns for Scottish independence.
1979	**first referendum on devolution:** slight majority in favour, but not enough voters to be valid (less than 40 % of the electorate)
1997	**second referendum on devolution:** strong majority in favour

Important stages in Scottish history	
1998	**Scotland Act:** specifying areas in which Scotland can make its own laws (vs. areas reserved for Westminster)
1999	The **Scottish Parliament** and the **Scottish Executive** (later **Scottish Government**) are established.
2011	The **SNP** win the **majority** in Scotland.
2014	**Independence Referendum:** Independence is supported by the Scottish National Party (SNP). The three main UK political parties (Conservatives, Labour and Liberal Democrats) make a public promise to devolve "extensive new powers" to the Scottish Parliament if independence is rejected. → **Independence is rejected** by a small margin (55 % against, 45 % in favour).
2016	**Scotland Act:** More powers are devolved to the Scottish Parliament and the Scottish Government (e. g. control over electoral system, onshore oil and gas extraction, Scottish income tax, etc.).
2016	After the **Brexit referendum**, in which a **majority** of the Scottish electorate (62 %) voted **for "Remain"**, the Scottish National Party (SNP) and its leader Nicola Sturgeon raise renewed **calls for Scottish independence within the EU**.

2.2   From Empire to Commonwealth

History of the British Empire and the Commonwealth

- **first overseas possessions and trading posts** under Queen Elizabeth I

- Britain's **rise to main colonial power** after controlling large parts of India (1757) and North America (1763)

- end of the "**First Empire**": losing the **American War of Independence** (1775 –1783)

- after loss of American colonies, new focus on **Australia**, **India** and **Africa**

- **19th century and early 20th century:** height of Britain's wealth and power: "**the empire on which the sun never sets**" (covers about one fifth of the world's land surface and rules over a quarter of the world's population)

- from the **end of the 19th century** and especially in the **course of the 20th century**, through a combination of violent protests and Britain's voluntary granting of power, **more and more countries** gradually become **independent**

- Imperial Conference (1926) and Statute of Westminster (1931): "**British Commonwealth of Nations**" as a community of equal and free member states who owe allegiance to the British monarch

- **London Declaration of 1949** officially founds the modern Commonwealth of Nations

- **today:** 56 member states; Charles III is Head of the Commonwealth, but head of state in only 15 of the member states; several states plan to become republics in the near future; three more recent countries to join the Commonwealth, Rwanda, Mozambique and Gabon, have no historical ties to the British Empire at all

Diverging views on the British Empire

	discussion topic
Positive impact	**Negative impact**
• "**progress**" and "greater good" (e. g. schools, hospitals, technological advancements in colonised countries)	• "progress" view based on **racist** and condescending attitudes (**cultural imperialism:** imposing of British culture destroyed other cultures)
• democratic structures, representative assemblies, rule of law, ideal of personal liberty introduced in different countries	• **apparent democratisation only achieved through force and violence** (e. g. support of slavery, ethnic cleansing of indigenous peoples, suppression of rebellions)
• for Britain, a time of great and unsurpassed **prosperity**	• **exploitation** of the colonies
⬇	⬇
"progress" view mainly from a Eurocentric perspective	**racism and brutality behind the Empire**

⬇

Consequences today:

- English as a **lingua franca**
- trigger for post-war **immigration** to Britain
- British **international influence** (seat on the UN Security Council); the **Commonwealth**
- **national pride** because of Britain's imperial past (problems with the EU / Brexit and problems with Scotland as a result of this attitude)
- controversy over the evaluation of the British Empire; the Black Lives Matter movement calls for a **critical examination of Britain's imperial past**

3   The UK's politics

- **constitutional monarchy:** a state form in which the monarch "reigns, but does not rule"; the monarch is bound to **parliamentary sovereignty** as well as to the rule of law
- **parliamentary democracy:** ≠ presidential democracy; leader of the government/executive derives their **power from Parliament**/the legislative
- **uncodified constitution:** The UK does not have a single document in which the constitution is laid down. Instead, the UK's constitutional rights are made up of **historical documents and conventions**, **statute law** (all acts passed by Parliament) and **common law** (court decisions).

The UK's political system

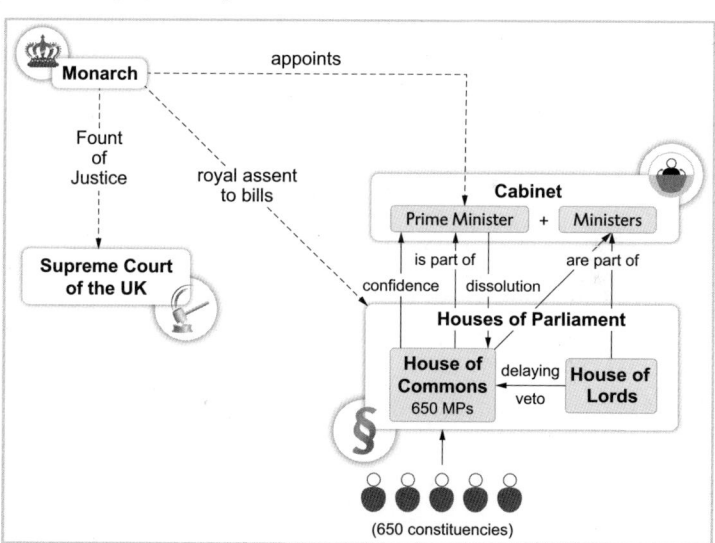

3.1 The UK's political parties

"first-past-the-post voting": simple majority voting system, ≠ proportional representation
In a constituency, only the candidate receiving the largest number of votes is the winner. All the votes for other parties are lost.
criticism: lack of representation, for example
candidate A: 35 % of all votes
candidate B: 34 % of all votes
candidate C: 31 % of all votes

➡ candidate A wins the seat, although more people voted against him/her than for him/her

- The UK is officially a multi-party system, but first-past-the-post voting favours big parties.
- The two main British parties are the **Conservatives** (Tories) and **Labour**.
- Since 1922, either the Conservatives or Labour have provided the British PM.
- The smaller British parties include: **Liberal Democrats**, **Green Party**, **Scottish National Party**, **Plaid Cymru** (Welsh nationalist party, left-wing), **Sinn Féin** (Irish republican party, against Irish separation), **DUP** (Democratic Unionist Party, Northern Irish anti-Catholic party, against Irish union), **UKIP** (United Kingdom Independence Party, strong supporters of Brexit, right-wing, nationalist).
- There has only been one **coalition** in recent history: Conservatives – Liberal Democrats (2010–2016).

Some facts about the UK's two big parties

Conservative Party	Labour Party
history: founded in 1834, emerged from the former **Tory Party**; before emergence of Labour, the Conservatives' main opponents were the **"Whigs"** (Liberal Party)	**history:** founded in 1900, traditionally linked to the **working class**

political position: centre-right	political position: centre-left
some political standpoints:	**some political standpoints:**
• free market economics	• governmental economic intervention
• critical of devolution	• taxation to support the redistribution of wealth
• socially conservative	• pro-devolution (but also pro-union)
• for a strong military capability	• tends to be socially liberal
important politicians: Winston Churchill (with an interlude for the Liberal Party), Margaret Thatcher, David Cameron, Theresa May, Boris Johnson	**important politicians:** Clement Attlee, Tony Blair, Jeremy Corbyn, Keir Starmer

3.2 British monarchy

The British monarch is **Head of State with representational functions**. They have no power to make laws. Their roles include:
- royal assent to all laws
- appointment and dismissal of prime minister and other ministers
- opening and dissolving of Parliament
- weekly audience with the prime minister
- Head of the Church of England
- Commander-in-Chief of the Armed Forces
- Fount of Justice (justice is carried out in the name of the monarch)

Public opinion of the monarchy in the UK

- Republicanism has always been a **minority opinion** in Britain, but it is usually stronger when members of the Royal Family interfere in political debate or are involved in scandals (e. g. Prince Andrew's involvement in a sex scandal, Charles as Prince of Wales a very outspoken supporter of environmental protection).

- Republicanism is generally stronger among the **younger generations** (survey 2021: 61 % in favour of the monarchy, but among 18- to 24-year-olds only 31 % in favour, 41 % against).

- "**Megxit**" = Duke and Duchess of Sussex (Prince Harry and Meghan) step down from their roles as senior royals in January 2020 amid allegations of racism in the Royal Family → loss of what used to be the most popular members of the Royal Family among the younger generation; harm to the public image of the Royal Family

- **Elizabeth II** usually kept to the functions circumscribed by the constitution and enjoyed a **great popularity** among the British population. → However, the popularity of her **successor**, King Charles III, is less certain.

Arguments for and against the monarchy

 discussion topic

Arguments for	Arguments against
• The monarch's position above party politics creates a **sense of continuity, unity and stability**. • The monarchy tries to be seen as **adaptable to modern society** and its values: e. g. Charles was allowed to marry a divorced woman, male children are no longer favoured in the line of succession. • Members of the Royal Family **head** many different **charities**, lending them their image and popularity. • The monarchy has an important function for the **tourism industry**: the international popularity of the British royals attracts tourists from all over the world. • The monarchy is a **connecting link to the former colonies** (monarch as Head of Commonwealth and official head of state in some Commonwealth countries).	• The monarchy is **inconsistent with democratic principles:** a head of state should be elected, not a function that is inherited. • The deference shown to the Royal Family **perpetuates inequality**, hierarchy and general unfairness (Britain as a "**class-ridden**" society). • The work the royals do is out of proportion to the **tax-payers' money they consume** and the advantages they get from their privileged positions. • The extensive **media coverage of trivial royal activities** diverts national attention from more substantial topics. • The Royal Family is **not representative of a modern (and multicultural) Britain** (e. g. close alliance to the Church of England, outdated gender roles, etc.).
the monarchy as a financial and political ("soft politics") asset for the UK	**the monarchy as an outdated institution that perpetuates the "wrong" values**

3.3   The UK and the EU (Brexit)

- **1973:** Britain joins the **EC** (European Communities, later to become the **EU**).
- EU membership has always been controversial in Britain ("**island mentality**", fear of losing the country's independence).
- The criticism comes to a head with the **financial and Euro crises** (2008/2009 and 2010–2012) and with **UKIP**'s anti-EU propaganda.
- **David Cameron**, a supporter of the EU himself, promises the British electorate a **referendum on EU membership** as part of the Conservative election campaign for the 2015 election.
- The **Brexit referendum** is held on **23 June 2016** and results in 52 % voting for "Leave" and 48 % for "Remain".
- Possible reasons for the outcome of the referendum are the following:
  - The two **big parties** are **divided** on the issue of Brexit (Labour pro-European, but also critical of the EU; Cameron himself pro-European, but enables the referendum to stop critics in his own party).
  - The "**Remain**" campaign is led with arguments **too far removed from people's everyday worries** whereas the "**Leave**" campaign is **based on populist and nationalist agendas** focusing on the glorification of Britain's imperial past ("taking back control") and an anti-immigration stance (in line with people's worries during the **migration crisis of 2015**).
  - A referendum appeals to **people's emotional decisions**, which are more cleverly manipulated by the "Leave" campaign.
  - The referendum reveals a **huge split in society** (along class and employment lines, along geographical lines, according to age, etc.).
- Cameron resigns and **Theresa May** takes over as prime minister in 2016.
- The **negotiations for a Brexit deal** take years and lead to several political crises and parliamentary blockades (May resigns in 2019 and is succeeded by **Boris Johnson** as PM).
- Brexit finally takes effect on **31 January 2020**.

- During the one-year transition period, the EU and the UK engage in fierce battles and finally sign the **EU-UK Trade and Cooperation Agreement** on 30 December 2020.
- The **future repercussions** of Brexit on the EU and particularly on the UK are still uncertain.

Arguments for Brexit and challenges connected with it

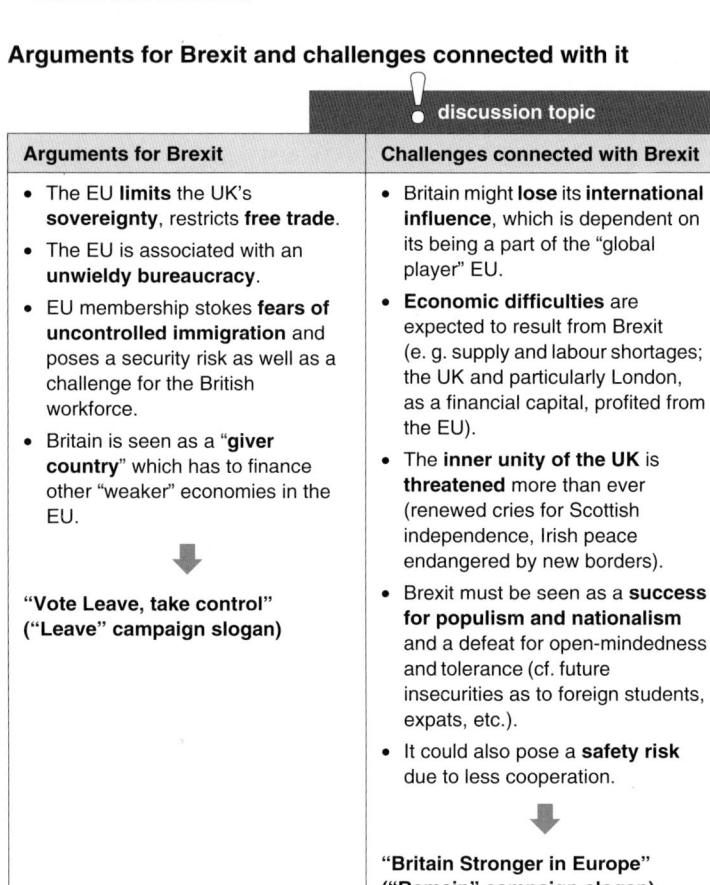

	discussion topic
Arguments for Brexit	**Challenges connected with Brexit**
• The EU **limits** the UK's **sovereignty**, restricts **free trade**. • The EU is associated with an **unwieldy bureaucracy**. • EU membership stokes **fears of uncontrolled immigration** and poses a security risk as well as a challenge for the British workforce. • Britain is seen as a "**giver country**" which has to finance other "weaker" economies in the EU. ⬇ **"Vote Leave, take control"** **("Leave" campaign slogan)**	• Britain might **lose** its **international influence**, which is dependent on its being a part of the "global player" EU. • **Economic difficulties** are expected to result from Brexit (e. g. supply and labour shortages; the UK and particularly London, as a financial capital, profited from the EU). • The **inner unity of the UK** is **threatened** more than ever (renewed cries for Scottish independence, Irish peace endangered by new borders). • Brexit must be seen as a **success for populism and nationalism** and a defeat for open-mindedness and tolerance (cf. future insecurities as to foreign students, expats, etc.). • It could also pose a **safety risk** due to less cooperation. ⬇ **"Britain Stronger in Europe"** **("Remain" campaign slogan)**

4 UK society

4.1 British (multicultural) identity

"**Britishness**" is a highly controversial term and cannot be clearly defined. Attitudes such as fairness, moderation and reserve, politeness, common sense and a distinctive sense of humour are often seen as typically British. The history of the Empire, a resistance against totalitarian powers as well as cultural and religious diversity could also be mentioned. In recent years, the term "Britishness" (or "Englishness") has often been exploited to serve nationalists in their vision of an ethnically uniform, White, English-speaking country, a vision that has never been true, not only because of more recent migration but also because of the United Kingdom's four nations with their unique English, Scottish, Welsh and Northern Irish traditions and roots.

Immigration to the UK

History of immigration	
19th century	**Irish** people escape poverty in rural Ireland, particularly during the **Potato Famine** (1845–1851).
1933–1945	Some **Jewish refugees** are accepted in Britain (e. g. Kindertransport scheme, 1938/1939), but there are also restrictions and even internments as "enemy aliens" during the war.
1948	**British Nationality Act:** gives people from (former) colonies the status of British citizens.
1948–1960s	Mass migration of **Commonwealth citizens** to Britain: The first of these are called the **Windrush generation**, named after the ship which docks in Tilbury on 22 June 1948, bringing workers from the West Indies.
1950s–1960s	Mainly **Asians** from the former British colonies of India, Pakistan and Bangladesh arrive in Britain.
2004 and following years	Migration from **eastern Europe** (e. g. Poland, Latvia, Estonia) after the **enlargement of the EU**
2015 and following years	**"Migration crisis": refugees/asylum seekers** (mainly from Eritrea, Iran, Pakistan, Sudan, Syria, Afghanistan, Iraq) seek shelter in the UK.

Reactions to immigration

Historically speaking, governments and societies have had different approaches to integrating immigrants into host societies:

- **separation:** This policy suggests that because ethnically diverse immigrants usually have little in common with the majority population, they should be kept separate.
- **assimilation:** This policy expects immigrants to lose their distinctiveness, such as their style of dress or belief, and adopt the customs of the host country.
- **pluralism:** This policy expects ethnic groups to participate and contribute to the host country, while at the same time maintaining their identity. Everyone in a pluralist society has the same rights and access to services. However, they are required to accept the society and actively participate.

- 1958: **Notting Hill race riots:** racially motivated riots in the London neighbourhood of Notting Hill → in answer to that, the **Notting Hill Carnival** has celebrated diversity (since 1959)
- strong **anti-immigration movement in the 1970s** (partly in reaction to Enoch Powell's "Rivers of Blood" speech in 1968)
- **1971: Immigration Act:** limiting immigration (especially from former colonies)
- **1976: Race Relations Act** and **Commission for Racial Equality** (later **Equality and Human Rights Commission** in 2007): attempts at anti-discrimination and more equality
- yet more **race riots**, e. g. in Brixton (London) and Toxteth (Liverpool) (1981): originate from protest against unfair police treatment of ethnic minorities
- **2005: suicide bombings on London public transport:** (in combination with 9/11 attacks in 2001) lead to widespread Islamophobia, but also to renewed debate about integration, because the attacks are carried out by "homegrown terrorists" (all four perpetrators had grown up and lived ordinary lives in the UK)
- **Brexit** motivated to a large extent by anti-immigration/nationalist mood roused by populist politicians

Multicultural Britain today

- About nine million people (or **roughly 14 % of the population**) in the UK are not White[2], but belong to other ethnically diverse groups.

- The largest of these are the **British-Indian**, **British-Pakistani** and **Black** (**African** or **Caribbean**) **British** people.

- The most ethnically diverse region in the UK is London, but other big cities, such as Bradford, Birmingham, Leicester and Nottingham, are also very ethnically diverse.

- Despite efforts and **programmes aimed at achieving equality and anti-discrimination** as well as the **success** of many people from ethnic minorities in business, the arts and entertainment, sports and also politics (e. g. Sadiq Khan, London's mayor of Pakistani descent), they still face **widespread disadvantages** in areas such as **housing**, **education**, **health care** and **employment**.

- The international **Black Lives Matter movement** has also started to highlight **police violence** and disproportionate **racial profiling** in the UK. Furthermore, a more thorough investigation into the **racist history of the British Empire** is often demanded.

- **Generational conflicts** between first-, second- and also third-generation immigrants also present urgent problems, e. g. conflicts between local and foreign customs, "homegrown terrorists" who, as later-generation immigrants, feel dismissed by UK society, lack orientation and become radicalised.

4.2 Class system in the UK

- The **social class** a person belonged to was traditionally based on **birth** alone, although today there are other defining markers, such as wealth, education and occupation.

---

2 The words "Black" and "White" are capitalised to signal that they are not natural categories but social ones (for more background information on this topic see for example https://www.theatlantic.com/ideas/archive/2020/06/time-to-capitalize-black-and-white/613159/).

- Traditionally, three social classes were distinguished: **upper class**, **middle class** and **working class** (with subdivisions, such as upper-middle class, lower-middle class, "underclass").
- It is a matter of debate whether the role of class is still as relevant in British society as it used to be because there is the **increased social mobility**.
- Yet, a number of arguments still speak for Britain as being a "**class-conscious**" or "**class-ridden**" society:
  - **monarchy**, **House of Lords** perpetuate the privileged position of the nobility
  - **public schools** (e. g. Eton, Harrow) and **elite universities** (e. g. Oxford, Cambridge) as breeding grounds for "**old boys' networks**" (the number of leading positions in business, politics, etc., filled by graduates of these schools and universities is disproportionate)
  - **RP (Received Pronunciation)** as a social, rather than a local accent (the way someone speaks is strongly connected to certain preconceptions and prejudices)
  - **strong class consciousness**, e. g. among the working class (stemming from the Industrial Revolution, times of trade union dispute during "Thatcherism", closures in mining and other heavy industries, …)

4.3   Religion

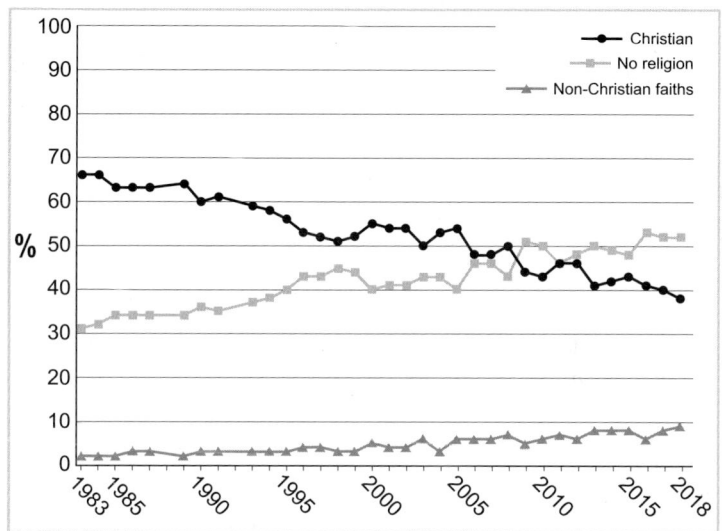

based on: "British Social Attitudes", © The National Centre for Social Research 2019

- Although the **Christian religion** is the dominant religion in the UK (the **Church of England** is even established as a **state church**), nowadays there are more people who see themselves as non-Christian than Christian in the country.

- In the context of traditional institutions, such as the **monarchy** or the **House of Lords** (with its Lords Spiritual), the church has an importance that is not represented in people's everyday lives.

- This is mainly reflected by the fact that fewer and fewer people go to church regularly and the UK has de facto turned into a largely **non-religious** country. According to surveys, this is mainly due to a **generational shift** with more and more young people not being religiously orientated.

- In contrast to Christian congregations, non-Christian faith communities, particularly **Buddhist, Hindu, Sikh** and **Muslim** communities are growing.

- **Religious tolerance** is an important value for many British people.

5 UK culture

science:
- British thinkers leading in moral/philosophical (John Locke, David Hume, Emmeline Pankhurst) and scientific (Isaac Newton, Charles Darwin, James Watt) inquiry
- some of the world's oldest universities (Oxford, Cambridge)

cinema and television:
- oldest surviving motion picture (1888)
- fierce competition, but also lively exchange with US film industry
- TV stations, such as BBC, ITV and Channel 4 known for their high-quality programmes
- renowned satire/comedy sector

performing arts:
- London's West End especially famous for its musicals, ballets and operas
- "The Proms" at Royal Albert Hall in London (classical music)
- festivals: Glastonbury (music/performing arts), Reading (world's oldest popular music festival), Edinburgh (world's biggest cultural festival)
- parades and carnivals ("Notting Hill Carnival")

sports:
- UK often referred to as "the birthplace of modern sport"
- cricket, football, rugby, tennis and golf, among others, originated in the UK

visual arts and architecture:
- pop art "vs." traditional fine arts, also subversive political art (Banksy)
- "fathers of the cartoon": William Hogarth, James Gillray
- Christie's (London) largest auction house in the world
- classical (e.g. Gothic, English Baroque, Christopher Wren: St Paul's Cathedral and many other London buildings) vs. modern architecture (e.g. Norman Foster: "The Gherkin", "Millennium Bridge")

culture and commerce:
- charity organisation National Trust as well as (partly) government-funded Arts Councils to preserve heritage and promote culture (for all social classes)
- free admission to national museums
- TV stations have a public service obligation, but also a commercial interest, especially those not funded by the government
- Does art have to be provocative? (cf. Banksy, punk rock, etc.)

influences:
- English, Scottish, Welsh and (Northern) Irish cultures
- cosmopolitan British culture (largely due to the UK's imperial history)

music:
- British classical music, but trailblazing especially in pop music
- 1960s: "British Invasion" (Beatles, Rolling Stones); British rock'n'roll, beat, British blues, rock, heavy metal
- 1970s: punk & new wave
- 1980s: "Second British Invasion": jazz, synthpop, Indie rock
- 1990s: boy and girl bands
- 2000s: soul
- increasingly also world music

cuisine:
- traditionally British dishes; e.g. roast beef, full English breakfast, meat pies, fish & chips, afternoon tea
- one of the most popular dishes today: Chicken Tikka Masala (cosmopolitan influences)

literature:
- prose fiction: invention of the modern novel in the UK (1740), novel still the dominant literary form
- drama: Elizabethan drama, "angry young men" and absurdist theatre after WW II, modern comedies and drama
- poetry: from Romanticism to modern forms of poetry (poetry slam, focus on women and minorities)

USA – between tradition and change

1 The USA's geography

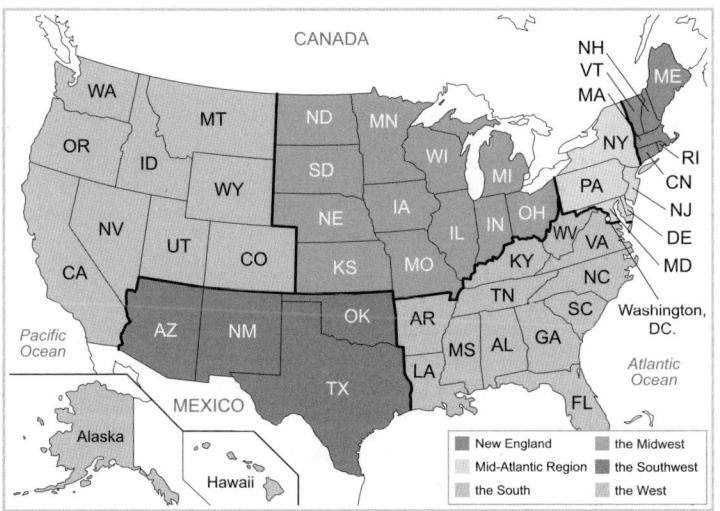

- **50 states** (48 contiguous), five insular territories (Puerto Rico, Northern Mariana Islands, US Virgin Islands, Guam, American Samoa) and minor possessions
- states often divided up into different regions with their own geographic and historic profile (see box in map)
- regions often associated with certain political attitudes, e. g. West Coast = "**Left Coast**", "**Bible Belt**" in the south
- **climate:** many different climate zones, generally warmer in the south, drier in the west
- major topographic features: **Appalachian Mountains** (east), **interior plains**, **Rocky Mountains** (west), **Great Lakes** in the north, four major **deserts** in the west and southwest (Great Basin, Mojave, Sonoran, Chihuahuan), major rivers: Mississippi, Missouri, Colorado

2 The USA's history

Aspects which are particularly relevant to African American history are highlighted in grey in the following table.

Important stages in US history	
~ 15,000 BC	arrival of **Native Americans**, who, in the following millennia, settle the whole area which is now the USA and form a variety of cultural groups
1492	**Christopher Columbus**'s arrival in the "New World", which is the starting point for centuries of colonisation and the destruction of Native American cultures
1607	**Jamestown**, Virginia, **first permanent colony** to be founded by English settlers
1619	**first African slaves** are brought to Jamestown (in the 17th century and particularly the 18th century, hundreds of thousands of Africans are enslaved and mainly work on tobacco and cotton plantations)
1620	**Plymouth Colony** is founded by the **Pilgrim Fathers**, who have arrived on their ship, the Mayflower, (mainly to escape religious persecution) → Massachusetts becomes the **Puritans'** new home
1773	**Boston Tea Party:** American colonists protest against British taxes by throwing tea from British ships into the harbour ("**no taxation without representation**")
1775–1783	**American War of Independence / American Revolution:** 13 American colonies (under the leadership of George Washington) fight British troops
1776	**4 July:** the **Declaration of Independence** is adopted
1787	the Founding Fathers draw up the new **constitution** for the United States of America
1789	George Washington is elected the **first president of the USA**
1791	**Bill of Rights** (first ten amendments to the Constitution): individual rights and freedoms for US citizens
1807	the **transatlantic slave trade** is **officially outlawed**, but the domestic trade continues

Important stages in US history	
19th century	**westward expansion** of the US: "**Manifest Destiny**" leads to Native Americans being displaced and killed in large numbers
~ 1830s–1850s	heyday of the **Underground Railroad:** organised escape of slaves from southern to northern free states
1854	opponents of slavery (abolitionists) set up the **Republican Party**
1860	Republican candidate **Abraham Lincoln** is **elected president**
1861–1865	**American Civil War** after eleven pro-slavery southern states seceded from the Union and formed the Confederate States of America
1865	after the defeat of the Confederates, **slavery** is **abolished** under the **13th Amendment**
1865–1960s	phase of **segregation** and "**Jim Crow laws**" in southern states (consolidated through Plessy vs. Ferguson court ruling, 1896: "**separate but equal**" facilities deemed constitutional)
1868	**14th Amendment:** US citizenship for all former slaves
1870	**15th Amendment:** right to vote granted to African American men
1917	the USA enters **World War I**
1920–1933	**Prohibition:** time span during which the sale of alcohol is illegal
1920	**19th Amendment: women** are given the **right to vote**
1924	**Indian Citizenship Act:** Native Americans are granted citizenship (although they remain ineligible to vote in some states until 1957)
1929–1939	**Great Depression:** period of economic downturn, mass unemployment and poverty, beginning with the **Wall Street stock market crash** of 1929
1933	President Franklin D. Roosevelt launches the **New Deal:** recovery programme which allows the government to partly regulate the economy
1941	the USA joins **World War II** after Japanese warplanes attacked the US fleet at Pearl Harbor, Hawaii

Important stages in US history	
1945	the USA drops two **atomic bombs** on Hiroshima and Nagasaki, Japan → Japan's surrender marks the **end of World War II**
1945	the USA as one of the founding members of the **UN** (United Nations)
1947	**Truman Doctrine** (the USA declares that it will support nations it deems threatened by communism): beginning of the **Cold War** with the Soviet Union
1949	foundation of the **NATO** (North Atlantic Treaty Organization)
1950–1953	US forces play a leading role against Soviet-backed North Korean and Chinese troops in the **Korean War**
1954	**racial segregation in schools** becomes **unconstitutional**
1955	**Montgomery bus boycott** in answer to Rosa Parks's refusal to give up her seat to a White passenger and her subsequent arrest
1957	enforced desegregation of **Little Rock High School**
1962	the Cuban missile crisis brings the USA to the brink of a nuclear war
1963	**March on Washington**; Martin Luther King Jr.'s **"I Have a Dream"** speech
1964	**Civil Rights Act:** aiming to halt discrimination on the grounds of race, colour, religion, nationality
1964–1975	American troops fighting in the **Vietnam War**
1965	Selma to Montgomery march; **Voting Rights Act**
1968	**Martin Luther King** is **assassinated**
1991	**end of the Cold War** (disintegration of the Soviet Union)
2001	**9/11 attacks:** suicide attacks by al-Qaeda terrorist organisation on World Trade Center and Pentagon → the USA embarks on a **"War on Terror"** that includes invasions of Afghanistan (2001) and Iraq (2003)
2002	creation of the **Department of Homeland Security** with far-reaching powers to fight terrorism

Important stages in US history	
2008	the major Wall Street **investment bank Lehman Brothers collapses**, marking the most serious economic crisis since 1929
2008	Democratic Senator **Barack Obama** becomes the first Black president of the United States
2013 onwards	the **Black Lives Matter campaign** begins on social media and turns into a global protest phenomenon against racially motivated police brutality
2016	**Donald Trump** is elected President
2021	**Joe Biden** is inaugurated as President amid stringent security measures two weeks after Trump supporters stormed the Capitol in Washington, D.C.

2.1 The USA's foreign policy: From isolationism to becoming "the policeman of the world"

Isolationist phases	Interventionist phases
after independence, policy of **neutrality and isolation** (Jefferson, 1801: "Peace, commerce and honest friendship with all nations, **entangling alliances with none**.")	
expansion to the west: **Monroe doctrine** (1823): US stays out of Europe, Europe stays out of America	
	1898: the USA fight on Cuba's side in the **Spanish-American War**; after Cuba's independence, the USA is given some Spanish possessions (Puerto Rico, the Philippines, Guam) → **USA as a colonial power** with overseas dependencies → Roosevelt: **need to interfere** in Asia or Latin America if national (economic) interests are concerned

World War I: President Wilson's commitment to remain **neutral**	the country gives up its neutrality and **enters the war in 1917** (after German submarine attacks) → plays a decisive role at the post-war peace conference → rise of the USA to a **global superpower**
return to isolationism after WW I; intense public debate: Should the USA be more involved in fighting fascist powers?	**1941:** Japanese attack on **Pearl Harbor** makes the USA enter WW II
	post-war efforts: • **Marshall plan** to rebuild a democratic Western Europe • USA as one of the founding members of the **UN** (intergovernmental organisation for global peace-keeping and international cooperation) • the USA has stabilised its role as a global superpower: **Cold War** in resistance to Soviet bloc (**Truman Doctrine**: "free peoples need our assistance")
	1990s: **reorientation after Cold War:** torn between global peace-keeping (UN / NATO interventions in Africa, Kosovo, etc.) and focus on its own economic and trade interests (e. g. in Kuwait)
	2001 terrorist attacks on USA → military interventions / **War on Terror** in Afghanistan, Iraq and worldwide

2.2 The terrorist attacks of 9/11

- 11 September 2001: terrorists hijack four planes and crash them into the twin towers of the World Trade Center in Manhattan, into the Pentagon in Arlington Country in Virginia and in a field in Pennsylvania (actually intended for Washington, D.C.)
- background: the **single deadliest terrorist attack** in recent history (almost 3,000 people killed and more than 6,000 injured), attack on American soil and against America's standing in the world
- consequences of the attacks:
  - new focus on **homeland security**: **Patriot Act** (**2001**): enhanced **domestic surveillance** and law enforcement techniques that would have been considered unconstitutional before the attacks
  - consciousness of being in a constant state of "**War on Terror**" (declared by President **George W. Bush** shortly after the attacks, "ongoing war" of a new kind: the enemy cannot be identified clearly)
  - detention camps (**Guantanamo**) for "**unlawful enemy combatants**" (not "prisoners of war", who would have certain rights) criticised as **gross violation of human rights** and stain on America's image abroad
  - **Islamic fundamentalism** is perceived as the main threat to the USA; **rise of xenophobia**/resentment especially against Arabs and Muslims/rise in **anti-Muslim violence** → tough immigration policy and a rise in deportations of illegal immigrants
  - **rise of fear and anxiety**; media perceived as transmitter and amplifier of these anxieties through reports of mass violence
  - **massive security measures** in air travel and at public events

3 The USA's politics

- **inauguration:** the ceremonial act of swearing the president into office
- **impeachment:** process by which a state official can be removed from office if they are convicted of unlawful or inappropriate behaviour
- **Super Tuesday:** unofficial name for the day on which many US states hold **primary elections** and thereby nominate their favourite presidential candidates
- **electoral college:** group of people who elect the US president; they are sent from all states (in varying numbers in proportion to the size of a state's population) and are chosen by popular vote (in most states through a "winner-takes-all" system)

3.1 Checks and balances in US politics

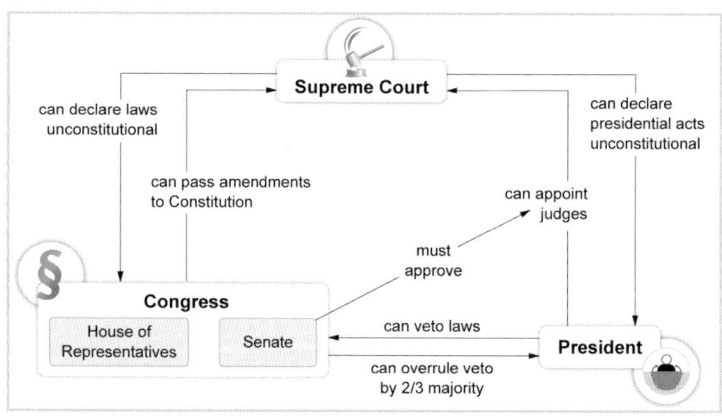

- **principle** of the US Constitution: powers are divided into **three branches of government** (executive, legislative, judicial) to prevent abuse of power, errors and fraud
- **President:**
  - forms the **executive** (together with his/her **Cabinet**)
  - elected for **four years**

- can serve a **maximum of two terms**
- elected by the citizens of the USA by **indirect vote** (via electoral college)
- very **powerful** role: both **Head of State** and **Head of the Executive**, **Commander in Chief of the military**, sometimes called a "substitute king" (but elected democratically, of course, not hereditary)

- **Congress:**
  - **legislative** branch
  - **House of Representatives: number** of members per state varies **according to a state's population**, members elected for **two years**
  - **Senate:** each state sends **two senators**, senators serve for **six years** and every two years one-third of the senators are up for election again

- **Supreme Court:**
  - **judicial** branch (together with smaller courts)
  - consists of **nine judges**, who serve for a **lifetime** and can only be impeached or resign voluntarily

Examples checks and balances

- The **president** can **veto** any bill passed by **Congress**, but a two-thirds vote in Congress can override the veto.
- The **president** can **appoint** the **Supreme Court judges**, but the **Senate** must **approve** these choices.
- **Congress** has **two chambers**, the House of Representatives and the Senate, who check on each other (both have to pass a bill before it becomes law).
- The **House of Representatives** has the sole power of **impeachment**, but the **Senate** is where an **impeachment trial** takes place.
- **Congress** can **amend the Constitution** and thus override the **Supreme Court**.
- The **Supreme Court** can **declare** the president's decisions **unconstitutional**.

3.2 The Democratic Party and the Republican Party

	Democrats	Republicans
Symbols:	colour blue	colour red
History:	founded in 1828, oldest political party in the world which is still active; historically rather conservative and supporter of economic liberalism	founded in 1854; historically the anti-slavery party
Basic political position:	liberal, more left-wing	conservative, more right-wing
Basic social ideas:	emphasis on community and social responsibility	emphasis on individual rights and justice
Some political standpoints:	• **higher tax rates** for higher income • mainly support for **gay marriage** • **abortion** should remain legal • **government regulations** are seen as necessary to protect the consumers • support for **universal health care** • **climate change** is considered a real threat • a pathway to citizenship for certain **undocumented immigrants** is supported	• **taxes as low as possible** for everyone • **military spending** should be increased • mainly opposed to **gay marriage** • **abortion** should not be legal • **government regulations** hinder free market and job growth • prefer **private healthcare solutions** • **climate change** is given rather low priority • support for **stronger enforcement measures at the borders**

Bildnachweis Esel / Elefant: © Kamigami / Dreamstime.com

4   USA society

4.1   The USA as an "immigrant country"

The USA is **one of the most culturally diverse countries** in the world. This is largely due to the fact that since its colonisation it has been "**a country of immigrants**". However, this designation has come under fire because it **overlooks both indigenous Americans and the experience of African Americans**. The former have been living in the USA since before colonisation, while the latter did not come to the country voluntarily, but were shipped there by force.

History of immigration to the USA	
early 17th century	**colonial immigration:** mainly British settlers arrive in the USA (first English colony: Jamestown, Virginia, 1607; Plymouth, Massachusetts, 1620)
17th/18th centuries	other early settlers from predominantly English, Scottish, German, Dutch, French descent
1790	**Naturalization Act:** allows any free White person of "good character" who has been living in the United States for two years or longer to apply for citizenship
~ 1815–1865	**first wave of immigration:** people from northern, western and central Europe (esp. 1840s: **Irish immigration**, almost half of all immigrants are Irish)
1848	**California Gold Rush →** Chinese immigrants are attracted in large numbers
1880–1920	**immigration peak:** 20 million immigrants (peak year 1907: 1.3 million people), also immigrants from central, eastern and southern Europe (Catholic and Jewish people add to the religious diversity)
1882	**Chinese Exclusion Act:** barring Chinese immigrants, first act in American history to place broad restrictions on certain immigrant groups
1892	**Ellis Island**, the United States' first federal immigration station, opens in New York Harbor

1924	**Immigration Act:** introducing **quotas** based on the percentage of people of the same nationality already living in the country in 1890 (this favours immigration from northern and western European countries)
1965	**Immigration and Nationality Act:** ends the national origin quotas → rising numbers of **Asian** and **Latin American** immigrants
1980s onwards	heated debate about **illegal immigration** in US politics (highest numbers of illegal immigrants from Mexico and other Central American countries)
2007	peak year of illegal immigration (12.2 million people, 4 % of total US population)

Immigration as a controversial topic in the US

	discussion topic
Arguments by opponents of immigration	**Possible counterarguments**
• **Security** argument: immigrants bring crime.	• Statistics prove that the **crime rates** among immigrants are **not higher**.
• Immigrants **take away jobs** from native-born workers.	• Immigrants often work in sectors where their **workforce** is **urgently needed**.
• Immigrants are a **burden on the budget**, the welfare system and the economy.	• Immigrants bring an **economic stimulus** and **increase in tax revenue** (even undocumented immigrants pay some taxes, but do not profit from benefits).
• Immigrants **endanger important cultural values** and social unity because of their different political and religious worldviews.	• Most immigrants show great **motivation to integrate** and identify with American values. **Multiculturalism enriches** American society.
⬇	⬇
irrational fears often exaggerated and exploited by populists	**American success story due to immigration to a large extent**

Melting pot vs. salad bowl

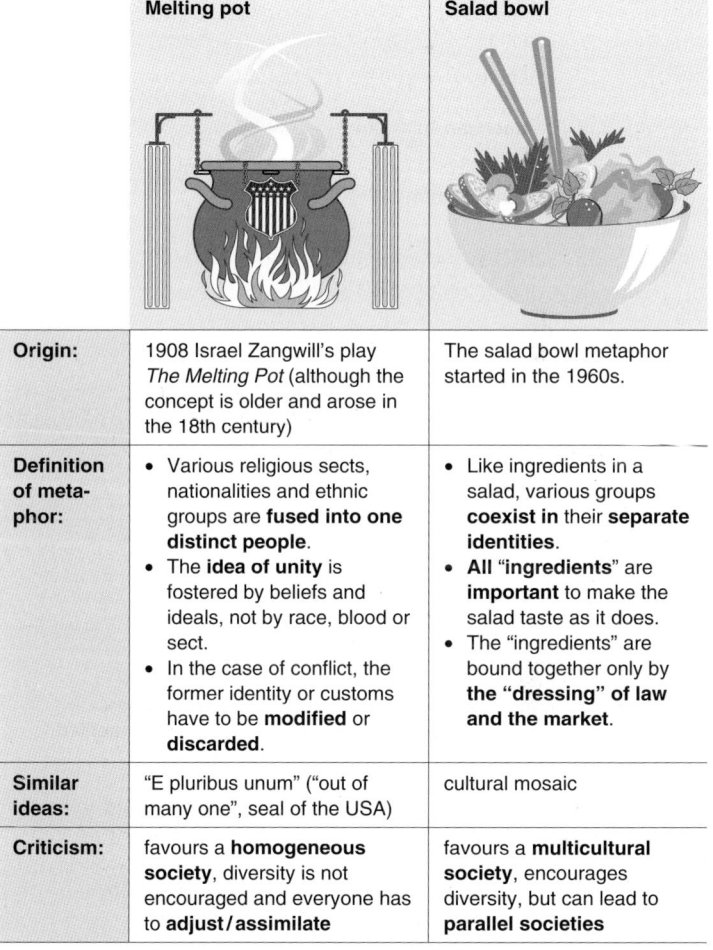

	Melting pot	Salad bowl
Origin:	1908 Israel Zangwill's play *The Melting Pot* (although the concept is older and arose in the 18th century)	The salad bowl metaphor started in the 1960s.
Definition of metaphor:	• Various religious sects, nationalities and ethnic groups are **fused into one distinct people**. • The **idea of unity** is fostered by beliefs and ideals, not by race, blood or sect. • In the case of conflict, the former identity or customs have to be **modified** or **discarded**.	• Like ingredients in a salad, various groups **coexist in** their **separate identities**. • **All** "ingredients" are **important** to make the salad taste as it does. • The "ingredients" are bound together only by **the "dressing" of law and the market**.
Similar ideas:	"E pluribus unum" ("out of many one", seal of the USA)	cultural mosaic
Criticism:	favours a **homogeneous society**, diversity is not encouraged and everyone has to **adjust / assimilate**	favours a **multicultural society**, encourages diversity, but can lead to **parallel societies**

4.2 The American Dream and other central concepts of American identity

American Dream

- **origin of the term:** James Truslow Adams (1931): "dream of a land in which life should be better and richer and fuller for everyone, with opportunity for each according to ability or achievement"
- **promises** from the beginning of colonisation:
  - **free land** and space
  - possibility of starting a **new life**, leaving everything else behind
  - opportunity of **self-realisation** to one's full capacity
  - society of **equal opportunities**, open to everyone independent of social status or origin
  - freedom to pursue one's happiness/**individualism**
  - recognition of the individual based on his or her achievements ("**meritocracy**")
- attractive to **immigrants** (cf. symbol of the **Statue of Liberty** and Emma Lazarus's poem, "The New Colossus", "Give me your tired, your poor, your huddled masses yearning to breathe free …")
- **popular myths and ideals:** "from rags to riches", "from dishwasher to millionaire", "the self-made man"
- main aspects:
  - **material well-being/economic success/prosperity**
  - social order offering **liberty, equality and political participation**
- American Dream or **American Nightmare**?
  - unlimited opportunities and space **at the Native Americans' expense**
  - **social mobility** and **equality** only a myth: USA one of the least socially mobile societies in the world (e. g. high cost of good education), (racial) minorities are not given equal opportunities
  - the ideology that hard work, sacrifice and risk-taking are the only prerequisites for prosperity/success can lead to self-blame for (maybe undeserved) failures and is used as a common argument against social security measures (**downside of individualism**: lack of solidarity/kind of ruthlessness)

"All men are created equal"

- one of the central statements of the **Declaration of Independence** (1776)
- Declaration of Independence made by slave owners (e. g. Thomas Jefferson): **contradiction** between the supposed equality of all human beings and the social/economic reality in the early republic
- lasting impact of the phrase, which is understood as **claiming equal rights and opportunities for every human being/American citizen** (cf. American Dream)
- **women's rights movement**, **Civil Rights Movement** and **Black Lives Matter** refer to the phrase to demand equal rights
- the equality of rights and opportunities is still not the case in US society: **formal equality but de facto discrimination** of certain groups (e. g. African Americans' disadvantages in education, housing, on the job market, etc.)

Manifest Destiny and frontier spirit

- phrase "Manifest Destiny" coined in **1845**
- idea that the United States is **destined by Providence**/God to spread **democracy, progress and freedom** (**American exceptionalism:** role model character of the USA, innate morality and value of the American democracy)
- motivated 19th-century US territorial expansion and was used to **justify the forced removal of Native Americans**
- **frontier** = the boundary between the area already settled by westward moving European Americans and "uncivilised" Native Americans' land; the term is also used to denote a certain **state of mind** ("**frontier spirit**"): courageous settlers encountering the unknown and living under very harsh circumstances but finally "mastering" the land
- **legacy of Manifest Destiny:** USA as "**global police**", self-proclaimed **leader of the "Free World"**
- **legacy of "frontier spirit":** celebration of **unapologetic individualism** (e. g. resistance to gun control, rejection of organised social security, etc.)

"Culture wars"

- The term was first used in 1991 to describe the **polarisation** of US society between people with values and lifestyles considered **traditionalist or conservative** and those considered **progressive or liberal**.

- Certain subjects are charged as **morally right or wrong** and exaggerated as defining "who we are".

- Typical "culture war" issues include:
  - abortion
  - homosexual and transgender rights
  - multiculturalism
  - gun ownership
  - patriotism and national symbols, such as flags or statues
  - religious beliefs and education (e. g. creationism vs. evolution)
  - welfare system
  - environmentalism

- Culture war issues are often (**mis**)**used in political campaigns**, because they can be intentionally exaggerated to **create in- and out-groups** and voters can be motivated to fight against a position on the other side of the political spectrum when they see their own identity and lifestyle threatened.

- "**Cancel culture**" is a controversial term often used by opponents of an allegedly exaggerated political correctness. It accuses those who want to deny potentially discriminatory opinions a public platform of limiting freedom of speech.

4.3 The USA and violence

Gun ownership and gun control

- Only a small **minority of US states** have strict **laws** restricting gun ownership (e. g. California, Illinois, Connecticut, New Jersey, New York, Hawaii, Maryland, Massachusetts).

- Gun ownership and gun control are very controversial issues, especially in the wake of **mass shootings**. Yet the **NRA** (**National Rifle Association**) and its supporters are against all types of gun control.

- 73 % of all killings in the USA are gun-related, compared to 4 % in England and Wales, 39 % in Canada and 22 % in Australia.
- Per 100 residents, there are 120 guns in the USA.
- historical background: **Second Amendment to the US Constitution:** "A well regulated Militia, being necessary to the security of a free State, **the right of the people to keep and bear Arms**, shall not be infringed."

Arguments of advocates and opponents of stricter gun control

discussion topic	
Advocates of stricter gun control	Opponents of stricter gun control
• The **Second Amendment is not an unlimited right** to own and carry guns, as it was linked to a "well regulated Militia". • More gun control laws would **reduce gun deaths** (also accidental deaths). Countries with restrictive gun control laws have lower gun homicide and suicide rates than the United States. • Guns are **rarely used in self-defence**. • The availability of weapons for everyone fosters a general **spirit of violence** and the perception of being constantly threatened by others.	• Gun control would **infringe** upon the **constitutional right** to bear arms. • Gun control laws do not deter crime; **gun ownership deters crime** ("The only way to stop a bad guy with a gun is a good guy with a gun."). • Gun control laws infringe upon the **right of self-defence**. This is contradictory to the American value of **individualism** (cf. "**frontier spirit**"). • Gun control laws are a means to control people and give too much power to the government (**guns supporting democracy**).
⬇	⬇
Unlimited gun ownership is dangerous.	**Limiting gun ownership means limiting freedom.**

Death penalty

- synonym: capital punishment
- About 60 % of all Americans support the death penalty.

- In more than half of all US states, capital punishment is still legal, although it is formally suspended in some of them.
- In contrast, the European Union is strictly opposed to capital punishment (the EU Charter of Fundamental Rights includes an absolute ban on the death penalty in all circumstances).

Arguments for and against the death penalty

 discussion topic

Arguments for	Arguments against
• It is an effective form of **deterrent** (without the death penalty, a state could be perceived as weak).	• According to statistics, it is **not** an **effective** form of **deterrent**.
• The death penalty is supposed to **cost** the government **less** than life imprisonment without parole.	• Mainly because of longer trials and more appeals, it is in fact **more expensive** than life imprisonment without parole.
• The death penalty is a **just punishment** for crimes that violate the victims' rights to life, freedom and safety.	• The death penalty is a form of **revenge**: its "eye-for-an-eye" mentality is **barbaric**.
• Modern methods of crime scene science can **effectively prove** someone's guilt or innocence.	• Innocent people might be killed (**miscarriages of justice**).
• It provides **closure** for the victims' families.	• It perpetuates an angry state of grief (**vicious circle of violence**).
• It offers convicted criminals **no chance of escape** and thereby **prevents** them from **repeating** their crimes.	• It offers **no chance of rehabilitation** for convicted criminals; mentally ill people might be executed instead of treated.
	• It is **racially biased** and **anti-poor** (Black people are more likely to be sentenced to death; a lot of money is necessary for a good legal defence).

death penalty seen as a "fair" punishment for some crimes

death penalty seen as inhuman

4.4 Religion

- In the USA, which is **officially a secular country** (the first officially secular country in western history even), **religion** plays a very **important** role. Both the country's secularity and its religiosity can be traced back to its history.

- The **First Amendment** to the US Constitution "provides that Congress make no law respecting an establishment of religion or prohibiting its free exercise." (**religious freedom**)

- This formulation is the result of the experience of the **first settlers** who often **fled religious persecution** in their home countries.

- The most famous example of this is the **Puritans**, who brought their Protestant beliefs and strict moral standards to America.

- Today, a similar form of religiosity is demonstrated by the **Evangelicals**, a fundamentalist movement among Protestant Christians who believe in the necessity of being born again ("spiritual rebirth") and the historicity of the Bible.

- Among **mainstream Christians**, religion also plays a more important role in everyday life than in European societies. In **rural areas** in particular, churches are at the centre of social and cultural life and offer many non-religious activities.

- Religion is also important in **politics**. Many political speeches close with "God bless America" or other kinds of religious wording and America is still referred to as "**God's own country**" (cf. the early settlers' idea of a "New Canaan" or "a city upon a hill" as a role model for others).

- Many of the country's **esteemed values** can also be traced back to an **early Protestant worldview**, e. g.:
  - self-reliance
  - hard work
  - perseverance
  - discipline
  - merit
  - decency

- Due to its predominantly Protestant history, this denomination is highly diversified. The most common Protestant groups are: **Baptists**, **Methodists**, **Lutherans**, **Presbyterians** and **Pentecostals**.

- Despite the religious freedom postulated by the Constitution, the **first non-Protestant immigrants** (Catholic Irish or Italian people, Jewish people) were often met with **prejudice**. In recent years, despite **religious tolerance** being a highly prized value, **anti-Muslim sentiment** has increased.

Religion in the USA

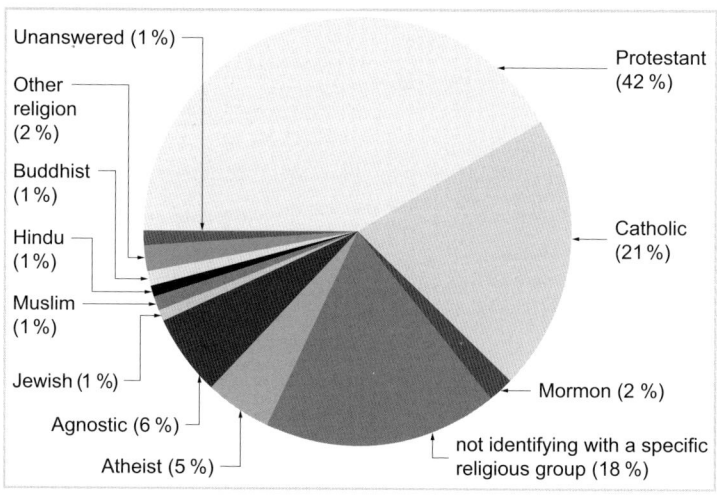

based on: "Measuring Religion in Pew Research Center's American Trends Panel". *Pew Research Center.* January 14, 2021.

5 USA culture

science:
- most Nobel Prize winners in the world
- most inventions of the 20th and 21st centuries either invented or first widely introduced in the USA
- many notable scientists immigrated to the USA (attraction of "land of the free")

music:
- music is one of the USA's most important contributions to the world's culture
- music styles which originated in the USA: country, jazz, swing, blues, rock'n'roll, techno, soul, hip-hop, among others (many of them influenced by African American musical traditions)

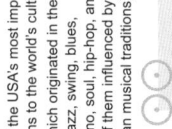

cinema and television:
- film as the American art form par excellence (Hollywood: oldest film industry in the world, largest in terms of revenue)
- largest television network in the world
- as early as the 1950s, half of all American households had a TV

culture and commerce:
- status of cinema and television particularly controversial because of their highly commercial nature ("infotainment", e.g. presidential debates, first to be televised: 1960)
- film and music in particular, but also other forms of culture credited with "Americanising" the world ("cultural imperialism")
- discussion about what constitutes art and what it is worth (cf. abstract paintings by Pollock or de Kooning which sold for several hundred million dollars)

sports:
- big focus on sports (e.g. college sports)
- sports originating from the USA: baseball ("the national pastime"), American football (most popular: "Superbowl" – most TV viewers), basketball
- usually among the top medal winners at Olympics

cuisine:
- great diversity
- iconic dishes: donuts, fried chicken, hamburgers, hot dogs, Thanksgiving turkey, pizza, burritos, tacos, "soul food" (influenced by what used to be "slave food" in the south)
- widespread obesity due to ubiquitous fast food restaurants

influences:
- originally, large English influence on American culture
- other European, Asian American, African American, Latin American, Caribbean and Native American influences (multicultural country)

visual arts and architecture:
- earliest "homegrown" American art: Hudson River School (19th century): motifs from nature. …
- later, abstract expressionism (influenced by Native American art), pop art, minimalism, postmodernism
- pioneering work in photography
- architecture: predominantly modern (skyscrapers), but also eclectically chosen European styles

performing arts:
- USA as the home of modern musical theatre (Broadway/ New York)
- stand-up comedy and improvisational theatre also originated in the USA
- opera, ballet, modern dance of worldwide fame (e.g. Metropolitan Opera)

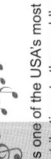

literature:
- poetry and prose: first golden age of American literature 19th century; since second half of the 20th century: increasingly, "minority" authors and themes (e.g. James Baldwin, Toni Morrison, Julia Alvarez, Sherman Alexie)
- drama: origin of uniquely American drama in the early 20th century (Eugene O'Neill), authors with mainly socio-critical themes include Edward Albee, Lorraine Hansbury, Tony Kushner

Global chances and challenges

Globalisation is the process by which the world is becoming **more and more interconnected**. This can be observed in different areas, such as **the economy and trade**, **culture** and **politics**. Furthermore, it affects the **environment**, often in a negative way. Changing patterns in **media usage**, especially the Internet (cf. chapter entitled "The media"), as well as modern means of transport can be seen as the biggest drivers of globalisation.

How globalisation changes the world

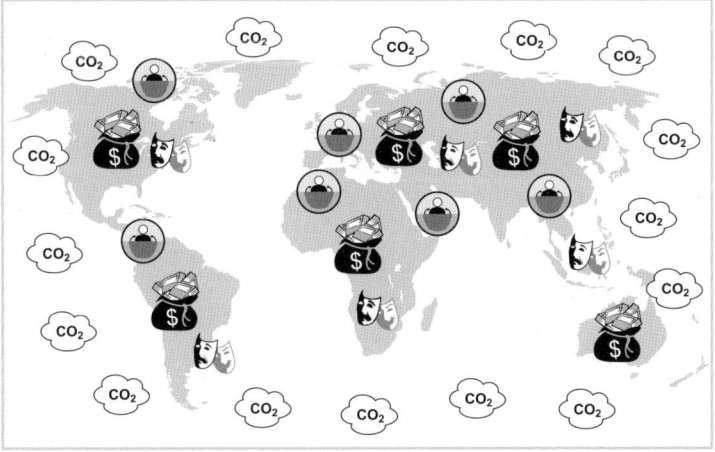

1 Globalisation and the economy

History of globalisation

- Even **ancient societies** (Greece, Rome) had trade connections extending as far as Africa and the Middle and Far East.
- In the **Age of Exploration**, European empires established colonies all over the world (15th century onwards).
- During the **Industrial Revolution**, an ever-increasing quantity of goods was transported far and wide.
- The **advance of technology**, especially in **transport** and **communications**, signalled the beginning of modern globalisation (starting after WW II). Accelerating factors were the end of the Cold War as well as the rising influence of the Internet.

Features of globalisation

- increased international **trade**
- **companies** operating in more than one country
- **dependence** of companies as well as national economies on the **international market**
- **freer movement** of capital, goods and services
- emergence of **global commodity chains** (stages of development, production, sales, marketing, etc. connected internationally) with **global assembly lines** (finished products assembled in several countries)

Example of a commodity chain

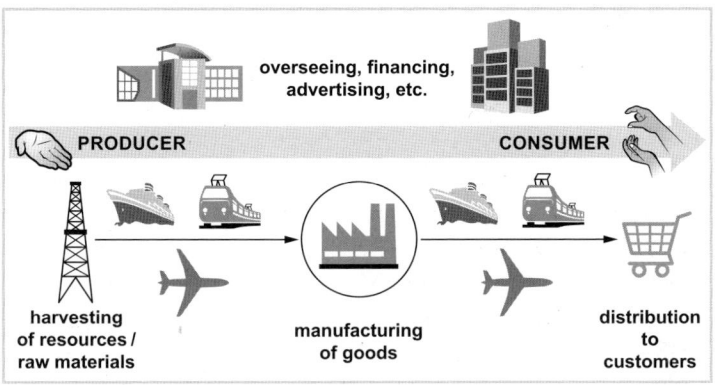

Factors speeding up globalisation

- **Freedom of trade:** Intergovernmental organisations, e. g. the World Trade Organisation (WTO), create a legal framework to overcome trade barriers between countries.

- **Improvements in transportation:** Goods and people can travel more quickly and more cheaply due to technological progress (e. g. air travel, large cargo ships).

- **Improvements in communications:** The Internet in particular has facilitated the communication between people and companies in different countries.

- Availability of **cheap labour and raw materials:** More economically developed countries (MEDCs) are attracted by cheaper labour costs and raw materials in less economically developed countries (LEDCs).

Positive and negative impacts of globalisation (economy)

discussion topic

Positive impacts	Negative impacts

• **Profitability:** at least some countries / companies can grow and develop. Ideally, profit will benefit all in the long run.
 	
• **Investments** of multinational companies **in LEDCs** can create **jobs** for local people and bring **wealth** and foreign currencies to local economies.
  → **Education, health care, infrastructure** could be built up in LEDCs.
 	
• **Exchange of ideas and experiences:** people can try products as well as lifestyles not previously available in their countries.
 	
• People become **more aware** of pressing international issues, such as global warming, the need for sustainable development, etc.
	• Widening **gap between rich and poor** countries: LEDCs are often exploited for the sake of MEDCs.
	
	• **Concentration of power:** multi-national corporations can use their enormous wealth and resources to control governments so that they act in their interests.
	
	• Despite legal frameworks, multi-national companies often operate with lower standards, which results in …
	  → **environmental pollution**
	  → **safety risks** and **poor working conditions** for local workers (e. g. in sweatshops)
	
	• **Unfair competition:** local companies are driven out of business by multinationals, which can produce more cheaply.
	
	• **Threat to diversity:** smaller businesses are lost (cf. chapter 3, "Globalisation and culture").
	
	• Due to the **dependence** on big multinational corporations, the world economy is **more vulnerable**.
	
	• Outsourcing leads to **job losses in MEDCs**, which can increase the potential for **xenophobia**.

 **globalisation as progress for all**	 **globalisation as a "one-way street"**

2 Globalisation and the environment

- New markets farther away lead to the **increased transport of both goods and people** (because of multinational companies' business travel).
    - More **greenhouse gases are emitted**, which contribute to **pollution**, **climate change** and **ocean acidification** and negatively impact **biodiversity**.
    - **Infrastructure**, such as roads and bridges, leads to **habitat loss** and **pollution**.
    - Transportation by ship heightens the **danger of major oil spills** or leaks that **damage the marine environment**.
    - Foreign animals, plants, fungi, viruses and bacteria can be brought to places where they can multiply without being checked (**invasive species**).
- The pressure of competition on the global market can lead to **economic specialisation** to heighten productivity and efficiency.
    - A focus on cash crops, such as coffee, cocoa or oil palms, can promote **habitat loss** for many plants and animals.
    - **Extensive cattle ranching** exacerbates **deforestation**, depletes soil and produces greenhouse gas emissions.
    - **Monocultures** can lead to **soil acidification** and **degradation**.
    - Fishing grounds are pushed beyond their biological limits (**overfishing**).
- **Energy production** has become increasingly global.
    - The enormous costs of prospecting for, extracting, refining and distributing oil and other fossil fuels have created an **oligopolistic market** where a very small number of companies dominate the industry.
    - Energy giants with enormous power influence governments to pursue policies in favour of fossil fuels and to **hinder the transition to renewable energies**.
- The global market is organised according to the interests of **consumer societies**.
    - **Mass market** production creates large amounts of **waste**.

- While there is **overconsumption** in some parts of the world, others experience shortages of existential goods. From a global perspective, the world economy **lacks sustainability**.

- **Human well-being** is threatened by the environmental changes. Unfairly, there is often a **disproportionate burden on less industrialised countries**.
  - Coastlines of tropical states are threatened by rising sea levels.
  - In some regions of the world, droughts and flooding are on the increase.
  - Health hazards are increasing due to malnutrition, lack of access to clean drinking water, etc.

- International travel, migration and global interdependence can also **raise awareness** for the effects of deforestation, habitat loss and climate change.

Positive and negative impacts of globalisation (environment)

discussion topic	
Positive impacts	**Negative impacts**
• Global connectedness can lead to **more awareness** of effects of globalisation. • **Concerted efforts, laws and regulations** are the only hope for long-term change.	• Increased **greenhouse gas emissions** negatively impact the world's **climate**. • Other negative impacts of global production are ocean and soil acidification, deforestation, **habitat loss** and **destruction**. • **Invasive species** can get out of control more easily. • **Biodiversity** is threatened. • **Human well-being** is **endangered** especially in LEDCs.
⬇	⬇
Climate change and other environmental issues can only be tackled on a global scale.	**Globalisation furthers overconsumption and non-sustainable economic practices.**

3 Globalisation and culture

Cultural globalisation means that **ideas**, **values** and **cultural products** cross borders. Due to the American dominance in that exchange resulting from the country's political and economic influence, some speak of a "**McDonaldisation**" or a "**coca-colonisation**" of the world.

Examples of "Americanisation"

- **Food:** Local diets and eating traditions are often drowned out by fast food giants. Fast food is popular, particularly among children, but also among adults who are increasingly pressed for time.
- **Film industry:** Powerful media conglomerates, which highlight Western notions of beauty, individualism and sexuality, drive a kind of "**cultural imperialism**". (While Bollywood is more prolific than Hollywood these days, Hollywood has the higher revenues.)
- **Music industry:** British and American pop music is listened to by young people around the world. (While Korean pop music / K-pop is catching up, for instance, it is still influenced by American musical styles.)
- **Clothing:** Both Western casual and business wear ("power suits") have become universal and symbolise modernity, independence and / or competence.
- **Consumption patterns:** The Western high-consumption lifestyle has spread around the world (e. g. shopping centres, leisure parks, car ownership, travelling, electronic devices, etc.).
- **Summary:** All in all, America seems attractive, especially to poorer countries, and can be a role model because of its power and prosperity and people's agreeable lifestyles.

Global consciousness

- An increase in global news coverage and communication (e. g. on social media) has led to a **more direct view** of events around the world.
- Similarities among cultures and shared values can lead to **better social relations**.

- Ideally, cultures **enrich** each other but maintain their individuality and local traditions that are worth preserving.
- People perceive themselves as **citizens of the world** and feel more involved in natural disasters or other events happening far away.
- However, the **opposite tendency** can also be observed: in times of crisis, people tend to withdraw into their local communities and expect (national) governments to protect them and solve the problem.

English as a global language

- A **lingua franca** is a means of communication for people from different linguistic backgrounds.
- For about 400 million people English is their mother tongue, while about one billion people speak English as a second language.
- English is the key language in business, science, politics, tourism and entertainment.
- Some experts claim that English is the world language because of its relatively easy grammar, but historical research has shown that a lingua franca mainly arises because of the **political, military and economic power** of the group or nation that uses it as their native language.
- History of English as a lingua franca:
  - The **British Empire** dominated a huge part of the world between the 17th and 20th centuries: English was institutionalised in schools, universities, the Civil Service, courts and business transactions, etc.
  - Even after the end of the British Empire, English remains a means of communication between different ethnic groups, e. g. in India.
  - From the middle of the 20th century onwards, the USA became **dominant due to its economy and culture**: English became the language used in finance, business, information technology, the Internet, film, television and music, etc.

Positive and negative impacts of globalisation (culture)

discussion topic	
Positive impacts	**Negative impacts**
• Shared norms and values can lead to **better social relations**. • Mutual cultural exchange can **spread knowledge and be enriching** for all. • A **lingua franca** facilitates **working and studying abroad**. • **Global consciousness** instead of **national egoism** can be furthered by recognising similarities.	• **"Cultural imperialism"**: A dominant culture drowns out individual local cultures. • The dominant culture is not necessarily of **better quality** (mass culture, fast food, etc.). • Dominance can also lead to **animosity**: if a culture or language is connected to suppression, people might reject it even if it could be enriching to their own culture.
⬇	⬇
mutual enrichment and global consciousness	**"levelling/dumbing down" & loss of individualism**

4 Globalisation and politics

Intergovernmental and supranational organisations

Intergovernmental organisations vs. supranational organisations: In supranational organisations, some powers of the member states are surrendered to the organisation, whereas in intergovernmental organisations, cooperation and coordination are voluntary.

- **Intergovernmental organisations**, e. g. the **United Nations** (**UN**), and **supranational organisations**, e. g. the **European Union** (**EU**), restrict the power of nation states through international law.

- International **non-governmental organisations** (**NGOs**), such as Amnesty International, Médecins sans frontières and Greenpeace, have a global outlook.

- **Aims of global political institutions** are to further economic co-operation, peace, freedom and democracy, but also to mitigate the negative effects of economic globalisation (cf. chapter 1, "Globalisation and the economy").

International terrorism

Terrorism is hard to define precisely. It comprises **unlawful acts of violence** which are intentionally **directed at civilians** to create fear and confusion. The perpetrators of these acts are often **radical groups that are religiously or politically motivated**.

- Since the **9/11 attacks**, many governments have started to focus on anti-terrorist measures. The Global War on Terrorism has been declared, but civil liberties have also been partly violated by surveillance laws that are meant to heighten security.
- Terrorism has taken on a new dimension due to globalisation:
  - Extremist groups often have an **extensive presence on social media** and can easily recruit and radicalise individuals.
  - Terrorists can **interact at the international level**.
  - Through the global interconnectedness of both people and places, terrorist attacks happen worldwide.
- However, global connectedness also offers the chance to **coordinate a global response** to terrorism.

Positive and negative impacts of globalisation (politics)

discussion topic	
Positive impacts	**Negative impacts**
• Global players (both governmental and non-governmental) might be in a position to **promote well-being, peace and democracy** worldwide. • **Global responses** are needed to find solutions for global problems.	• Global organisations tend to be bureaucratic ("**red tape**") and out of touch with people's lives. • **Radical groups** can easily connect and **influence** large groups of people.
⬇	⬇
Globalisation offers the chance to improve the world.	**Globalisation can both estrange people from politics and bring them into closer contact with it.**

The media

- **media:** tools of communication across space and time
- **person-to-person communication** (e. g. by post, telephone, email, messenger services) vs. public communication (via **mass media**, e. g. newspapers, radio, TV, Internet)
- **one-to-many communication** (traditional mass media) vs. **many-to-many communication** (interactivity of the Internet)

1 History of the media

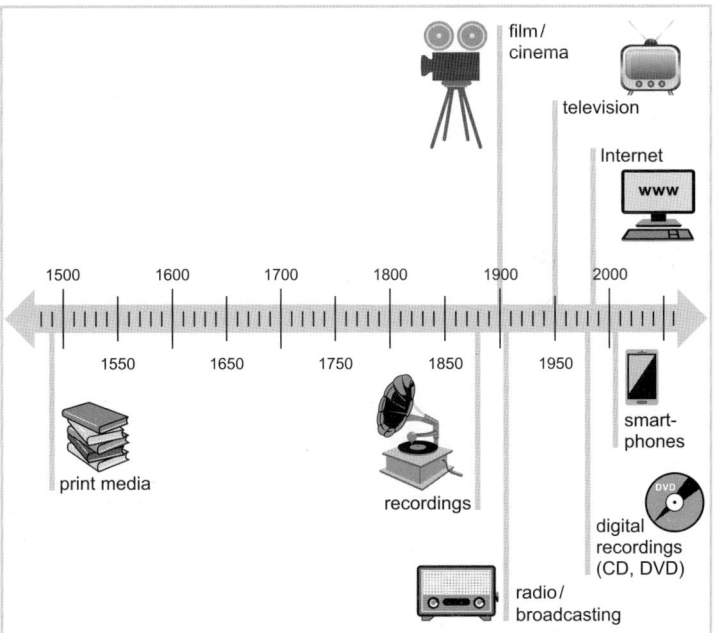

2   Traditional media

Print media in the UK were traditionally divided into:
- **broadsheets/quality papers** and
- **tabloids/popular press**

Today, the close connection between format and standard of quality has been more or less lost.

- The 19th century marked the beginning of **print media as a tool of mass communication**. This was mainly due to two reasons: better education of the masses, i. e. **more people learning to read**, and cheaper printing methods, which allowed the sale of newspapers at **cheaper** prices.

- The transition of the print media to a tool of mass communication is often hailed as an important step towards **democratisation**. The **freedom of the press** is an important basic right in democratic states (cf. the First Amendment to the US Constitution, for instance). As what is called the "**Fourth Estate**" (besides the executive, legislative and judiciary), the media fulfil the important democratic functions of:
  - **information** (and thereby empowerment) **of the masses**
  - **control of those in power** (e. g. exposure of President Nixon's involvement in the Watergate scandal, 1972; Edward Snowden's revelations about secret services, 2013)

- However, the media's powerful role has also been **criticised** for multiple reasons:
  - The downside of providing the public with as much information as possible has led to a **lack of respect for the individual's right to privacy** (e. g. Rupert Murdoch's *News of the World* hacking scandal in 2011).
  - As most media publishers have a **commercial interest**, this has often led to a so-called "**dumbing down**" of content to appeal to as wide an audience as possible.
  - Some politicians tend to be more interested in their **entertainment value** and **media effectiveness** than in their political programmes because of the media's decisive influence on the voters (cf. "**spin doctors**" who "orchestrate" politicians' performances).

– In their efforts to achieve a high circulation through **sensationalist reporting**, the media are often accused of **scaremongering, populist writing** and **dividing society**.
– As the biggest media outlets are often **concentrated in the hands of a few very powerful individuals** (not seldom with connections to political parties), it is unclear whether there really is such a thing as **unbiased and neutral reporting**.

3   Media literacy

A **critical approach to media consumption** is necessary, especially in view of the influence of mass media. The ability to consume media critically is called media literacy.

Aspects of media literacy

Facts to be aware of	Important questions for critical perception
The media do not simply represent the real world, but reconstruct it and present their own version of reality.	• **Who** produced the media product? • **To what purpose** was it produced?
The meaning of any kind of media product **depends on how consumers perceive it.** Differences in age, gender, ethnicity and social background influence people's reactions.	• Do I have a similar background to the people depicted or does it differ? How does this **influence my reaction**? • How might a person from a different background see this product?
The media have **commercial implications**.	• **How** can someone **make money** with this product? • In what way does this **influence** the product?

The media convey certain **ideas of what is right and what is wrong**, what is good and what is bad, who you can believe and who you can't.	• **Who / What** is shown in a **positive / negative light**? **Why?** • **Who / What** is **left out**? **Why?** • **How credible** is the portrayal? • What **other opinions** might be possible?
The content of a certain product partly depends on the **format of the medium**.	• What **mode of presentation** is possible in a certain medium? • What is the **effect of certain techniques** (e. g. lighting, camera angles, arrangement into chapters, etc.)?

4   The digital age

Types of digital media:
- **websites**
- **social networking** (some of the most popular social networking sites include Facebook, Instagram, Twitter, LinkedIn, Snapchat and TikTok, etc.)
- **email**
- **blog** (web log)
- **vlog** (video blog)
- **podcasts**
- **RSS feeds:** (RSS = rich site summary, really simple syndication), a kind of news ticker that can be subscribed to and provides its subscribers with the latest updates on a website (e. g. news headlines)
- **video games:** games that can be played on a computer, either alone or with other players (gaming community can also be a kind of social network)

Digital literacy

- The age of digital mass media presents consumers with a particular array of **challenges**, for instance:
  - The Internet offers an **overwhelming and often cumbersome amount of information** on any topic.
  - **Anyone can contribute** to the Internet, which can make it hard to judge the quality of entries.
  - Sources/copyright owners are often difficult to trace back, particularly as many contributions are added **anonymously**.
  - Both the **number** and the **diversity** of the contributions multiply the views propagated on the net. This can be positive, but also challenging, especially when views are radical and/or (deliberately) false ("**fake news**").
  - A special problem is posed by what are called "**filter bubbles**", i. e. algorithms that choose what to show Internet users based on their former preferences. That way prejudices and opinions are confirmed and people can easily form a one-sided and biased view of the world.
- That is why **digital literacy** requires skills in addition to "normal" media literacy skills, such as:
  - the skills to **search** the Internet **effectively** and **filter** information **sensibly**
  - the skills to **compare and evaluate** different sources successfully
  - the awareness regarding the "digital footprint" one leaves on the Internet and the necessity to **protect sensitive data**
  - the awareness to ensure that **copyright laws** are not violated
  - **respect for diversity** and **polite interaction** (despite the anonymity of the Internet)

Opportunities and challenges connected with the Internet (and social media)

discussion topic

Opportunities	Challenges
• The Internet can support **diversity** and connect people with different perspectives around the globe. • It allows people to **stay in touch** and interact with friends, family and others irrespective of distance. • It facilitates **international cooperation.** • Digital contact can be beneficial for the **environment**. It reduces the need for **business travel**, for instance. • The Internet permits a **more flexible approach to work** (mobile working). • It can be **empowering** for people because it offers easily accessible information for all. • New modes of contact can foster **creativity and innovation** because companies can access consumer data directly.	• The Internet can cause **division and strife** because of anonymous communication and "**filter bubbles**" that foster **tribalism** and **hate speech.** • It can easily be **manipulated** ("fake news", hacking, trolls). • The Internet and social media can become **addictive**. • **Empathy, meaningful communication and relationships** are believed to suffer when lives are lived digitally. • Social media can negatively impact both the **physical** and **emotional well-being** of users (lack of physical activity, pressure through constant comparison, spiral of negativity). • There are **data security concerns**. • The **constant availability** of the Internet could make a healthy work-life balance more difficult.
The Internet can bring people closer together and make their lives easier.	**The Internet is not always a free, democratic and pleasant place.**

Science and technology

1 Biotechnology and genetic engineering

- **biotechnology:** branch of science dealing with the use of biological organisms or their parts in different fields of application, such as medicine, agriculture or industry
- **genetic engineering:** also called genetic modification or GM; the manipulation of genomes to obtain certain desired characteristics. Genomes can be manipulated by genes being transferred from one organism to another or being removed, or by DNA being created synthetically.
- **GMOs:** abbreviation for genetically modified organisms, i. e. organisms whose genes have been manipulated by means of biotechnology

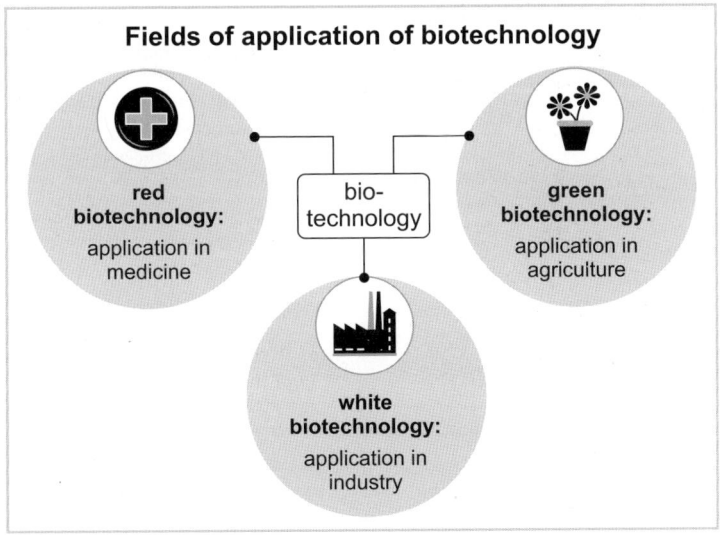

Fields of application of biotechnology

red biotechnology:
application in medicine

bio-technology

green biotechnology:
application in agriculture

white biotechnology:
application in industry

1.1   Green biotechnology

- the application of biotechnology in **agriculture**
- main aim: to make agriculture more efficient by **breeding more resistant crops** or **crops with a higher nutritional value**

Example

Golden Rice: Wild rice is modified to produce beta carotene, which is needed by humans to make vitamin A. Golden Rice can be cultivated in areas where vitamin A deficiency is common.

Hopes and fears connected with green biotechnology

	discussion topic
Hopes	**Fears**
• Traditional selective breeding takes a long time. Genetic modification is **a faster and more efficient way** of getting the same results.	• **Genes might spread uncontrollably** to other species and cause undesirable or harmful changes (e. g. "superweeds" that are resistant to herbicides).
• **World hunger** might be **alleviated** through crops with high nutritional value.	• **Biodiversity could be reduced** if GM plants push out other species.
• If more pest-resistant plants could be bred, **fewer herbicides would be necessary**, which would lessen the strain on the environment.	• GM crops could cause **farmers' dependence on the biotech industry**.
• Agriculture could become less risky if the **dangers of climate change**, disease, pests, etc. could be **weathered by GMOs**.	• GM crops could be **harmful to human health**, for instance by causing allergic reactions or otherwise impacting the **consumers' organisms**.
⬇	⬇
a solution for pressing agricultural problems	**a further burden on ecosystems**

1.2 Red biotechnology

- the application of biotechnology in **medicine**
- subareas:
  - **genetic testing/genetic screening:** examining DNA to predict diseases
  - DNA **paternity tests**
  - DNA profiling in **crime investigations**
  - **pharmacogenomics:** attempts to individualise medications to patients' (genetic) needs
  - **genetic engineering** to eradicate diseases or make organisms produce substances needed
  - **stem cell research** (see below)
  - **therapeutic cloning** (see below)

Stem cells

- Stem cells are unspecialised cells that can grow into any type of cell found in the body. There are two types of stem cells:
  - **adult stem cells** – can develop into many (but not all) types of cell
  - **embryonic stem cells** – can develop into any type of cell
- Adult stem cells come from grown-up individuals and are extracted from special tissues, such as bone marrow. Human embryonic stem cells can be removed from unused embryos "left over" from fertility treatments, for example.
- The main (intended) uses of stem cell therapy are:
  - **research** on diseases and medicine (on cells in the laboratory and not on actual patients)
  - the **replacement of defective cells or organs** with functioning ones

  Example

  Parkinson's disease: Experiments with mice have been successful in creating new brain cells that Parkinson's patients lack.
- Despite its potential, there are **social and ethical concerns** about the use of human embryonic stem cells, especially if stem cells are taken from embryos that are specifically created for these purposes and destroyed by the treatment.

Cloning

- **reproductive cloning:** creating an exact replica of a whole organism
  → Human reproductive cloning has so far been banned throughout the
  world. However, the theoretical possibility of human clones is often
  a subject of dystopian novels (cf. chapter 3.1).

- **therapeutic cloning:** the creation of only certain cells or organs that
  are required medically (usually from the embryonic stem cells of a
  cloned embryo) → Therapeutic cloning is allowed in most countries
  under very strict regulations.

Opportunities and risks of human cloning

	discussion topic
Opportunities	**Risks**
• **Infertile people** or **same-sex couples** could have children made from cloned cells. • Clones can be **sources of organs** or tissue for **transplantation**. • **Medication** can be **tested individually**. • **Desired characteristics** can be reproduced.	• It **infringes** upon everyone's **human rights** (including those of embryos) if they are "produced" for a certain end, e. g. to be a source for organ transplantation. • Human beings' **exclusive identity** is threatened by reproductive cloning. • Gene editing could lead to "**designer babies**", which could in turn make **society** look down on certain individual traits (and flaws) as being **unwanted**. • In horror scenarios, people could be "**bred**" for certain purposes by those who control the gene-editing process (through **money or power**).
⬇	⬇
progress and healing (esp. with regard to therapeutic cloning)	"**playing God**" (esp. in the dystopian sense of "breeding" human beings)

1.3   White biotechnology

- the application of biotechnology in **industry**
- attempts to make products or create energy in a **sustainable** way (especially relevant in times of environmental destruction and the rapidly diminishing supply of non-renewable energy sources)

Examples

- research on **biodegradable plastic**
- production of **energy from biomass**

2   Artificial intelligence (AI)

artificial intelligence (AI) = intelligence shown in machines as opposed to natural intelligence shown in living creatures
One aspect of their "intelligence" is that AI systems can **react to their environment** as well as **learn and progress** from earlier decisions.

Examples

- facial recognition software
- online shopping algorithms
- translation services
- search engines
- digital assistants, such as Siri or Alexa
- self-driving cars
- chess computers

Opportunities and risks that come with AI

	discussion topic
Opportunities	**Risks**
• AI can make **workplaces safer**: AI can do dangerous or hard work or scan workplaces for possible dangers.	• AI can take away people's jobs when they are replaced by robots, which leads to **unemployment and poverty**.

- AI can make life **more comfortable and efficient** by suggesting tailor-made products and activities.

- AI could be good for the environment **avoiding wastefulness** through targeted predictions of people's needs or "smart cities".

- AI can **help people with disabilities** to lead more independent lives and can fill vacancies in nursing and health care.

- AI can solve some tasks **more quickly, more efficiently and on a larger scale** (e. g. chess computers).

- AI can **perform certain high-precision tasks better** than human beings, because factors such as nervousness, fear and tiredness, etc., do not interfere (e. g. surgical robots, self-driving cars).

- AI could be used to **overcome biased judgements** (e. g. in job interviews).

- AI **endangers privacy** if collected data is sold to companies or used by criminals for unauthorised transactions.

- AI could have an **unhealthy influence** on people's lives if treated as "real". Real human contact could be neglected.

- AI could **make humans themselves less capable** because they could rely too much on machines.

- **Limits of AI** have to be recognised: they are not capable of **creativity**, **critical thinking** or **curiosity**, for example.

- AI could run out of control and become **dangerous** if it were used in critical situations (e. g. as a weapon or in self-driving cars) precisely because **it lacks human morals, critical thinking or empathy**.

- AI can **repeat or even exacerbate human bias** or prejudices because it is taken for an objective decision-maker although it is **only as good as the data it is fed** (e. g. hiring algorithms preferring male applicants to female ones, policing software identifying ethnic minorities as "higher risks", etc.).

AI is only the logical next development to come after robots and other machinery to make our lives easier.

Limitations of AI need to be taken seriously and the uniqueness of the living brain recognised.

3 Future worlds in literature

3.1 Utopia – dystopia

- **utopia:** an **imaginary society** in which people live a **happy life** in a perfect environment, governed by just laws
- **dystopia:** an **imaginary society** in which people live an **unhappy life** in an unjust system and are often ruled by a repressive state

- Sir **Thomas More** coined the word "utopia" in 1516 when he used it as the title for his book, in which he imagined a perfect community set on an island.

- The word is derived from the **Greek *ou-topos***, meaning '**no place**' or '**nowhere**'. The almost identical Greek word ***eu-topos*** means '**good place**'. So, More was already alluding to the question of whether a thoroughly good world can really exist.

- Every utopia carries within it the germ of a **dystopia** and sometimes the boundaries between the two can be fuzzy: what is perceived as a perfect society may vary from person to person. So, when **uniform values** are forced upon everyone, this can be regarded as dystopian.

- The **heyday** of literary dystopias has been both **the 20th and the 21st centuries**, after having experienced **totalitarian societies or states** (although there are also earlier books which can be included in that genre and often deal with social problems – in response to the Industrial Revolution, for instance).

- One of the main **characteristics** of dystopian novels is that they present **pessimistic views of the future**. These are usually connected to a **political message**, i. e. the alternative societies in dystopias mostly have a threatening and repressive government. Furthermore, dystopias' principal aim can be seen in **exaggerating existing negative tendencies** in order to criticise and warn of them.

- **Typical dystopian topics** include (most dystopian novels deal with several of the following themes):
  - the mechanics of **repressive societies** and **censorship**

  Examples
  - George Orwell, ***Nineteen Eighty-Four*** (1949): The protagonist Winston Smith lives in an imaginary future Britain, in which a totalitarian government closely controls all aspects of its citizens' lives. By rewriting history and changing language, even people's thoughts are to be influenced. When Winston falls in love with Julia and begins to rebel against the totalitarian society, he has to face the full brutality of the regime.
  - Ray Bradbury, ***Fahrenheit 451*** (1953): The society in which *Fahrenheit 451* is set is one that despises all forms of individual and critical thinking, which is why owning books is forbidden. The protagonist of the novel, Guy Montag, works as a fireman, whose job it is to find and destroy still-existent books. When he gets closer to Clarissa, a kind of rebel against the society's conformist views, he begins to question his job and the ideology behind it.

  - the influence of **technology** on humans

  Example

  Dave Eggers, ***The Circle*** (2013): Mae Holland finds a job at the Internet giant "The Circle", which advertises total transparency on the net. While Mae at first believes in the promises of "The Circle" to create a more open, friendly and safer society, she gradually realises her own growing addiction to the world of social networks as well as the downsides of complete transparency.

  - **surveillance** and a loss of privacy

  Example

  Suzanne Collins, ***The Hunger Games*** (2008): The powerful Capitol stages so-called "Hunger Games" every year, in which teenagers from twelve subjugated districts have to fight each other and only one of them can survive. Their fight for survival is filmed and transmitted live to the Capitol audience.

– human **cloning**/artificially created life

Examples

- Aldous Huxley, ***Brave New World*** (1932): The society of *Brave New World* is based on the principle that every citizen is "bred" for a certain purpose, i. e. for a certain social status. Combined with an entertainment society, the happiness drug "soma" and a certain view of history, people should be able to lead completely carefree, but also completely meaningless lives.
- Kazuo Ishiguro, ***Never Let Me Go*** (2005): Several human clones learn that they were only created as organ donors for the humans they were cloned from. The question of what makes humans human is a central theme of the novel.

– the **loss of individualism** and meaningful relationships

Examples

- Margaret Atwood, ***The Handmaid's Tale*** (1985): In a society where the ability to bear children has become rare, the few women still able to do so are enslaved and deprived of their individuality. Offred, the protagonist of the story, wants to be more than a breeder for the children of the powerful.
- Lois Lowry, ***The Giver*** (1993): In the fictional society of the novel, "Sameness" has become the norm, i. e. people have been deprived of all emotions, positive and negative, to guarantee social order. 12-year-old Jonas is chosen as a "Receiver of Memory" and is consequently given access to the whole range of emotions, which he experiences for the first time in his life.

– industrialisation/the **exploitation of nature and people**

Example

H. G. Wells, ***The Time Machine*** (1895): The protagonist is a nameless time traveller, who, on one of his journeys, lands in a future society, in which the social hierarchy of working and ruling class has been put to an extreme: the carefree Eloi seem to be served by the Morlocks, who live underground in darkness and squalor. However, in fact, the Eloi have to live in constant fear of the actually more powerful Morlocks.

3.2 Science fiction

Science fiction is a genre of fictional literature, the content of which is **imaginary** yet **based in science**. In other words, it relies on scientific facts, theories and principles to support its settings, characters, themes and plotlines, although it inflates these facts and thereby tells unrealistic stories.

- "Sci-fi" has many different subgenres and often shows utopian or dystopian features, so there is no clear-cut distinction between the genres.

- Another difficult distinction to make is that between science fiction and **fantasy**. In contrast to "sci-fi", fantasy commonly has no basis in real, scientific or technological facts or inventions.

- The list of "sci-fi" themes is quite similar to dystopian fiction, but can be more specifically grouped under the heading of "science and technology", for instance:
  - cloning
  - genetic engineering
  - computers
  - artificial intelligence (AI)
  - robots
  - environmental problems and climate change
  - space and time travel
  - alien life forms

The English-speaking world – between tradition and change

1   Ireland

1.1   Country profile

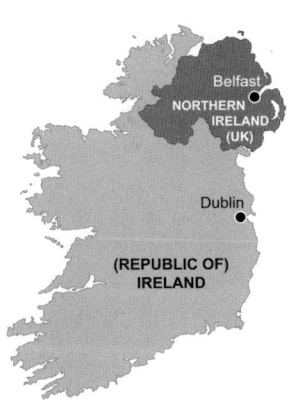

- official name: Éire (Irish/Gaelic), Ireland (English); **geographically**, "Ireland" refers to the island to the west of Great Britain, which **politically** comprises "The Republic of Ireland" and "Northern Ireland" (part of the UK); together with Great Britain, Ireland forms the **British Isles**

<u>**Republic of Ireland**</u>

- capital: **Dublin** (almost 40 % of the population live in or around Dublin)
- official languages: Irish, English; English is more widely used, but **Irish** is the **first official language** (roughly 11 % speak it as their mother tongue, mainly in the **Gaeltacht** areas in the west of the country)
- population: roughly 5 million (approx. 63 % urban, 37 % rural)
- area: roughly 70,000 km²
- population density: roughly 72/km²
- monetary unit: euro
- climate: dominated by the Atlantic Ocean, mild winters, moderate summers, a lot of rain throughout the year → **"Emerald Isle"**
- economy: mainly based on the **service industries**; mining, manufacturing and construction also remain significant; **agriculture**, the country's backbone in former times, produces only 2 % of the GDP but still plays an important role (five out of the country's seven million hectares of land are used agriculturally)

- political system: **parliamentary democracy:** two-chambered parliament (**Dáil** and **Seanad Éireann**/Senate), Dáil elects the prime minister (**taoiseach**), president with mainly representative functions
- religion: Celtic traditions and symbols still present in Irish culture, but **Roman Catholicism central to Irish identity** (especially due to its connection to Irish nationalism and the resistance to British rule); yet, declining numbers (close to 98 % of Roman Catholics in the 1960s, about 78 % today)

1.2   History

Important stages in Irish history	
5th century	**St Patrick**, who is later to become the patron saint of Ireland, begins the island's **christianisation**.
1171	Henry II of **England claims authority** over Ireland.
16th/17th centuries	The **English Reformation** brings religious persecution to Irish Catholics, many of whom flee the country and are replaced by English and Scottish Protestants, especially in the north of Ireland ("**Ulster plantation**").
1690	**Battle of the Boyne:** Protestant William of Orange beats Catholic James II, which results in further discrimination against Catholics.
1801	**Act of Union:** The United Kingdom of Great Britain and Ireland is established.
1845–1849	**Irish Potato Famine:** About one million people die, about two million emigrate.
from second half of the 19th century onwards	The support for an Irish independence movement/for **Irish Home Rule** grows. The **Fenian Movement**, predecessor of the **IRA**, is founded.
1916	**Easter Rising:** A violent rebellion to enforce Irish Home Rule is brutally crushed by the British.
1919–1921	**Irish War of Independence:** The IRA (Irish Republican Army) successfully employs guerilla tactics.
1921	**Anglo-Irish Treaty: Ireland is partitioned** into the Irish Free State and Northern Ireland, which chooses the option of remaining in the UK.

Important stages in Irish history	
1922/1923	The **Irish Civil War** between supporters and opponents of the treaty is won by the more moderate pro-treaty group.
1937	The Free State adopts the name of **Éire** and a new constitution.
1949	Ireland finally becomes a **republic**, severs all ties with the British monarchy and leaves the Commonwealth.
1969–1998	**Troubles** in Northern Ireland: The violent conflict between Catholic republicans and Protestant unionists lasts for decades.
1973	Ireland becomes a **member of** the EC (later to become the **EU**).
1995	**Divorce** is legalised.
1998	The **Good Friday Agreement** (Belfast Agreement) ends the decades of fighting during the Troubles.
2015	**Gay marriage** is legalised.
2018	**Abortion** is legalised.
2020	**Brexit** presents the problem of a potential new hard border between the Republic of Ireland and Northern Ireland.

1.3 Ireland today and in the future

- **Immigration and emigration:** The country has always had a high rate of emigration, which is shown for example, in the reaction to **British rule** or the **Potato Famine**. The number of people with Irish ancestry outside Ireland by far exceeds the Irish population "at home", with 70 million people worldwide claiming Irish heritage. However, Ireland is also attractive to immigrants (especially since the country's EU membership and **economic boom years**): about 12 % of the population are from ethnic minorities.

- The "**Celtic Tiger**": From the mid-1990s to the late 2000s, Ireland experienced unprecedented economic growth, but in the aftermath of the economic crisis of 2008, this growth came to a halt again.

- **The declining influence of the Catholic church:** Reasons for the decline in religiosity can be found in rising economic prosperity, a more secular lifestyle and the emancipation of women, as well as in revelations about child abuse in the church.

- Ireland's **increasing liberality:** cf. **history of abortion:** Abortion was only legalised in 2018. Before that, Ireland had very strict abortion laws. Many women travelled to the UK or other countries to have an abortion. The life of the foetus used to be considered as valuable as the life of the mother until 2013, so even in cases where a woman's life was endangered, a termination of the pregnancy was illegal.

- **Brexit and Ireland:** A potential hard border between the Republic of Ireland and Northern Ireland has led to fears of newly emerging violence, which is why, according to the Northern Ireland Protocol, Northern Ireland is to remain part of the single market and of the UK customs territory. However, the Protocol is not undisputed.

- **Irish culture:** While Ireland's **musical tradition** is legendary (e. g. traditional folk music and dance), the country is also well known for its **literature** with **four Nobel prize winners** in this field (1923: W. B. Yeats, 1925: George Bernard Shaw, 1969: Samuel Beckett, 1995: Seamus Heaney). Irish culture is popular throughout the world (also due to the "**Irish diaspora**"). For instance, Irish pubs can be found in many cities and St Patrick's Day is celebrated throughout the world on 17th March.

2 India

2.1 Country profile

- official name: Republic of India/Bharat Ganraya
- capital: New Delhi
- official languages: Hindi, English; (thousands of ethnic groups with hundreds of unofficial languages)

- population: more than 1,400,000,000, **second largest population in the world** (approx. 36 % urban, 64 % rural, with Mumbai, Kolkata and Delhi three of the largest urban areas in the world)
- area: roughly 3,287,000 km², seventh largest country in the world
- population density: roughly 464/km²
- monetary unit: Indian rupee
- climate: mainly tropical, influenced by the **monsoon**
- economy: about half of the workforce makes a living directly from **agriculture**; however, **high-technology**, trade, finance and services are the largest contributors to the GDP → development of a highly-educated middle class (but only about 20 % of the workforce in the "organised" and highest-grossing sectors of the economy)
- political system: **largest democracy in the world**, two houses of parliament, president, vice president, council of ministers (headed by the prime minister)
- religion: more than 75 % **Hindus**, largest religious minority: **Muslims** (approx. 17 %), also Christians, Sikhs, Buddhists, Jains, Jewish people, different groups of animists, etc.

2.2 History

Important stages in India's colonial and postcolonial history	
16th century	European nations establish trade with India.
16th to 19th centuries	Starting with the **East India Company**, Britain gradually expands its rule over India.
1858	The British Crown takes direct control after a rebellion of Indian soldiers ("Indian Mutiny").
1858–1947	**The Raj:** Britain rules the Indian subcontinent.
1876	Victoria I adopts the title "**Empress of India**".
1885	The **Indian National Congress** is founded as a political party to promote Indian independence from British rule.
after World War I	**Indian hopes for independence** grow stronger. → The British initially react with brutal repression (e. g. **Massacre of Amritsar**, 1919).

Important stages in India's colonial and postcolonial history	
1919 onwards	The Indian National Congress leader **Mahatma Gandhi** urges his Indian compatriots to resist British rule by non-violent forms of protest, such as boycotts or non-cooperation (e. g. Salt March, Quit India Campaign).
1947	The **Indian Independence Act** abolishes colonial rule and creates **two states**: India (with a Hindu majority) and Pakistan (with a Muslim majority). → Riots and migration ensue.
1947/48	**First Kashmir War:** The border region is violently disputed between India and Pakistan (two further wars follow in 1965 and 1999).
1948	**Gandhi**, who advocated a multi-faith India, is **assassinated** by a Hindu fanatic.
1950	The new constitution comes into effect and India is the **first Commonwealth country to become a republic**.
1980	The **BJP** (Bharatiya Janata Party) is founded and makes **Hindu nationalism** socially acceptable.
1991	A **free-market economy** is introduced in India, which leads to strong economic growth.
2012	After the **Delhi gang rape and murder**, India changes its laws regarding rape and gender-based violence.
2019	The **Citizenship Amendment Act** is passed by the BJP-dominated parliament amidst heavy protest due to its alleged discrimination against Muslims.

2.3   India today and in the future

- **Caste system:** The caste, or *jati*, is a strongly regulated group into which one is born. Castes regulate **social status, marriage and occupation**. There are thousands of *jatis*, but they are grouped into **four main social classes** called *varnas*: 1. *Brahmans* (priests), 2. *Kshatriyas* (warriors, landowners), 3. *Vaishyas* (merchants), 4. *Shudras* (artisans and labourers). Castes with no *varna* designation *(dalit)* used to have a very low social status and were considered to be "impure" and therefore "untouchable". **Officially**, the caste system has been

abolished and there are even attempts at positive discrimination to promote people from lower castes. However, it has retained some influence, especially in rural areas.

- **Tensions between groups of the population:** Since the partition of India, there has been **ongoing conflict** between India and Pakistan, especially in border regions such as Kashmir, which both countries claim as being part of their own territory. Within the country of India itself, recent years have seen a growth of **Hindu nationalism** (including under Prime Minister, Narendra Modi).

- **Overpopulation, gap between rich and poor and between city and country:** In the megacities especially, sanitary problems, such as inadequate sewage and garbage disposal or polluted water supplies, lead to unhealthy living conditions and diseases. However, more and more people are migrating from rural areas to the cities in the hope of profiting from India's economic growth and because problems like illiteracy and poor health care are often worse in rural areas.

- **Largely patriarchal family structures:** Family is the most important social unit, especially in the countryside. **Marriages** are often still **arranged** by family elders and the obedience of wives to their husbands is a strong social norm. Men generally have a higher social status than women and daughters are often seen as a liability because they require dowries. Even though the **gender inequality** has lessened in recent years, there is still a gap between men and women with regard to **education** and **social rights**. **Violence against women**, while officially condemned, is common, especially in domestic circumstances.

- **Indian culture:** India has a rich cultural heritage, including its world-famous architectural masterpieces like the Taj Mahal, for instance, but there are also many cultural exports from the food and clothing sectors, the fine arts, dance, music, literature and the cinema (e. g. "**Bollywood**" as the world's most productive film industry). While both the entertainment industry and the country's literature have been "westernised" to a degree, there are also typically Indian influences and literature in Indian languages. Rabindranath Tagore, who wrote both in English and in Bengali, was the first non-European to win the Nobel prize for literature in 1913.

3 South Africa

3.1 Country profile

- official name: Republic of South Africa
- nickname: the "**Rainbow Nation**" (indication of the country's multi-cultural diversity: approx. 80 % Black South Africans from different cultural and linguistic groups, White South Africans mainly of Dutch and English origin, Asian South Africans mainly of Indian and Chinese descent, multiracial South Africans)
- capitals: Pretoria (executive), Bloemfontein (judicial), Cape Town (legislative); (largest city: Johannesburg)
- official languages: **eleven official languages** (Zulu, Xhosa, Afrikaans, English, Sepedi, Setswana, Sesotho, Xitsonga, Swati, Tshivenda, Ndebele)
- population: roughly 60,000,000 (approx. 67 % urban, 33 % rural)
- area: roughly 1,221,000 km^2
- population density: roughly 49/km^2
- monetary unit: South African rand
- climate: warm, temperate climate, relatively dry, cooler in higher regions
- economy: most industrialised, technologically advanced and diversified economy in Africa; **third largest economy in Africa** (after Ni-

geria and Egypt); approx. 70 % **services**, but also **natural resource extraction** as an important sector of the economy

- political system: **parliamentary republic** (still member of Commonwealth, but does not recognise the British monarch as Head of State): power is shared by the president, who is both head of state and head of the government, and parliament consisting of two houses (National Assembly and National Council of Provinces)
- religion: predominantly Christian (approx. 80 %) with many independent African Christian churches combining traditional African religions with Christian beliefs

3.2 History

Important stages in South Africa's colonial and postcolonial history	
1652	The **Dutch East India Company** establishes a settlement in what is now Cape Town. → Dutch settlers come into conflict with local indigenous groups.
1795/1806	The **British** seize the **Cape Colony** from the Dutch.
18th/19th centuries	**Xhosa and Zulu Wars:** conflict between Dutch or English settlers and indigenous peoples as well as between different groups of indigenous peoples
early 1800s	Dutch "Voortrekkers", who resent British control, found their own **Boer Republics:** the South African Republic (now Gauteng, Limpopo, Mpumalanga, North West province), the Natalia Republic (now KwaZulu-Natal) and the Orange Free State (now Free State).
1867/1884	**Diamonds** and **gold** are found, which leads to even more efforts by the colonisers to push back the indigenous population as well as to more conflict between Boers and English settlers.
1880/1881 & 1899–1902	**Boer Wars** end in defeat of the Boers. Their republics become British colonies.
1910	The **Union of South Africa** becomes an independent dominion of the UK.
1948	The **National Party** wins elections and officially establishes **apartheid** (although segregation and discrimination have been common before).

Important stages in South Africa's colonial and postcolonial history	
1948–1990	**Apartheid era:** The population is grouped into three categories: "Whites", "Indians and Coloureds" and "Blacks". Racial **segregation** and **discrimination** particularly against the Black majority: forcible relocation into "**homelands**", disenfranchisement, prohibition of "mixed marriages", widespread segregation, etc.
1960	The anti-apartheid party **ANC** (African National Congress) is declared illegal.
1961	South Africa becomes a **republic** and is more or less forced to leave the Commonwealth due to its apartheid policy.
1970s/1980s	Resistance against apartheid grows, but protests, such as the **Soweto uprising** (1976), are brutally crushed and "Black Consciousness" leaders, such as **Steve Biko**, are killed (1977).
1986	**Global sanctions** against South Africa are put in place.
1990	**Nelson Mandela**, one of the leaders of the ANC, is released from prison after 27 years. He and President F. W. de Klerk are set to **dismantle apartheid** and transition to majority rule.
1994	**First free and democratic elections:** Mandela becomes president and de Klerk his deputy. South Africa rejoins the Commonwealth.
1996	The **Truth and Reconciliation Commission** starts its hearings to come to terms with apartheid and its aftermath.
2010	South Africa hosts the **FIFA World Cup**.
since 2016	The **Prevention and Combating of Hate Crimes and Hate Speech Bill** is controversially discussed as a means to fight discrimination on the one hand and an instrument to limit free speech on the other.

3.3 South Africa today and in the future

- **The legacy of apartheid:** Since the end of apartheid, both the political and social situation have **improved** for all South Africans. Still, **prob-**

lems like violence, crime, poverty, a lack of adequate housing and education, unemployment (rate of over 25 %), etc. **persist** and disproportionately affect the Black section of the population.

- **Vicious circle of poverty:** Particularly in some townships, **poverty and crime** are still rampant. A lack of adequate education results in very high numbers of unemployed, which in turn causes frustration and quite a high level of **violence and crime**. Coupled with **harmful gender roles**, both gender-based violence and teenage pregnancy are not uncommon. These problems perpetuate the vicious circle of crime and poverty and compound the AIDS crisis.

- **Accountability and justice:** Mandela's vision for the "new" South Africa was one of **reconciliation** instead of the Black majority taking revenge for their unfair treatment during apartheid. That is what the **Truth and Reconciliation Commission** was about: both victims and perpetrators were invited to speak out about injustices done to or by them. Perpetrators would then be granted **amnesty** instead of being punished. While this idea has been hailed as an exemplary way to avoid the perpetuation of violence, not everyone was as enthusiastic, and a **deep-rooted mistrust** between the different parts of the population lives on to a certain degree.

- **AIDS pandemic:** 20 % of all people infected with HIV live in South Africa. As it is mainly people aged 15 to 49 who are infected (about one in five), the pandemic hits the **economic backbone of the country** and results in many children becoming **orphans**. Prevention has been inconsistent for a long time, with even politicians denying the seriousness of the spread. While the government now finances a large part of the HIV response and provides millions of patients with anti-retroviral treatment, infection rates still remain high.

- **South African culture:** Due to the ethnic and social diversity, there is quite a **varied cultural mix** in South Africa. Famous musicians and bands that fuse a variety of influences include Ladysmith Black Mambazo, Miriam Makeba († 2008), Hugh Masekela († 2018) and Johnny Clegg († 2019) and Savuka. South Africa has two **Nobel Prize winners for literature**, Nadine Gordimer (1991) and J. M. Coetzee (2003), who both write in English.

4 Nigeria

4.1 Country profile

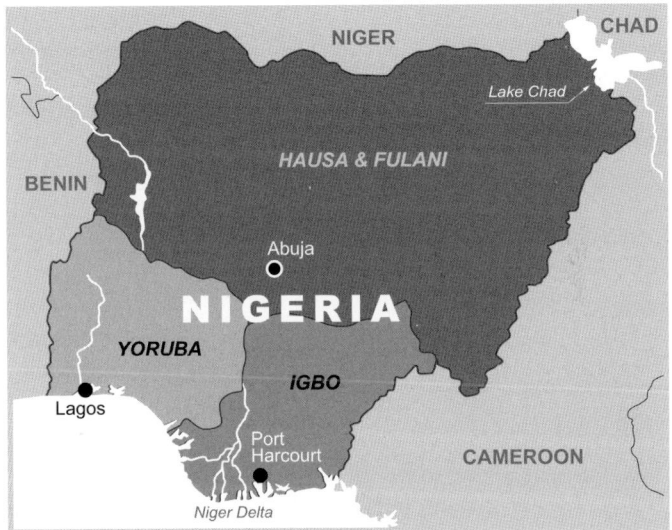

- official name: Federal Republic of Nigeria
- capital: Abuja (since 1991, founded as a **compromise** between conflicting ethnic groups); main commercial and industrial city: **Lagos** (between 15 and 21 million inhabitants, one of the fastest-growing cities in the world)
- official language: English (but more than 250 ethnic groups with different languages, e. g. Yoruba, Igbo, Fula, Hausa)
- population: over 215 million (Africa's **most populous country**) (approx. 52 % urban, 48 % rural)
- area: roughly 924,000 km^2
- population density: roughly 226/km^2
- monetary unit: Nigerian naira
- climate: varied with tropical climate in the south, savanna and steppe climate with danger of **desertification** in the north

- economy: **largest economy in Africa**; part of the "Next Eleven" (countries identified for their economic potential); most important sector of the economy is resource extraction, above all **crude oil** (also natural gas, coal, gold, etc. though these industries are still underexploited); financial and technological hubs, especially in the south; approx. 30 % employed in agriculture, but **population growth** too big to remain self-sufficient
- political system: **federal republic** (American model): president, head of state and chief of the executive, National Assembly consists of the House of Representatives and the Senate, three systems of law: common law, customary law and Sharia law (in the north)
- religion: about half of the population **Muslims** (especially **Hausa** and **Fulani** in the north, some **Yoruba** in the southwest), slightly less than half **Christians** (especially **Igbo** in the southeast, some **Yoruba** in the southwest), small percentage of followers of traditional religions

4.2 History

Important stages in Nigeria's colonial and postcolonial history	
17th/18th centuries	**Height of slave trade in Nigeria:** The slave trade is mainly run by Portuguese and British slave traders and partly supported by indigenous kingdoms.
late 19th century	The **British** colonise Nigeria in the face of fierce resistance by indigenous kingdoms.
1914	The **Southern and the Northern Nigeria Protectorates** are merged under British rule, but there are still different levels of interaction between the colonisers and the colonised (more interaction in the south than in the north, divide-and-rule policy by the British).
1960	Nigeria becomes **independent** and a new constitution is established.
1963	Nigeria becomes a **republic**, but remains a member of the Commonwealth.
1963–1966	**First Republic**
1966	A **military coup** ends the First Republic.

Important stages in Nigeria's colonial and postcolonial history	
1967–1970	The Igbo declaration of an independent "**Republic of Biafra**" causes the Nigerian **Civil War**.
1970s	An **oil boom** occurs.
1975	Another military coup initiates a transfer of power.
1979–1983	**Second Republic**
1983	Another **military coup** ends the Second Republic.
1983–1993	Different **military regimes** hold power.
1993	Short existence of the **Third Republic**, which is again toppled by a military coup.
since 1999	**Fourth Republic**
since 2009	The **Islamist terrorist group Boko Haram** is increasingly attacking the north and the middle of the country in particular.

4.3   Nigeria today and in the future

- **Religious and ethnic tension:** Even after their defeat in the Civil War in 1970, there are still **secessionist movements** among the Igbo. Furthermore, religious **tension between Muslims and Christians** tends to flare up from time to time, especially in the middle belt of the country. The radical group **Boko Haram** is trying to establish a Muslim theocracy in Nigeria, with both Christians and Muslims suffering as a result of their terrorist attacks.

- **Unequal distribution of wealth:** Although the country profits hugely from the oil trade, a large section of the population has to deal with very **low living standards** (approx. 40 % live below the poverty line). This is attributed to political incompetence as well as **corruption** and **overpopulation**. Furthermore, it is often **foreign or multinational oil companies** that profit most, not the Nigerians themselves.

- **Overpopulation:** Infrastructure and other services tend to have difficulty catching up with the rapid population growth. Particularly in big cities, huge **slums** with inadequate sanitary facilities are a consequence of this massive growth and of internal migration.

- **Environmental problems:** The dependence of the country on oil has led to non-sustainable harvesting practices. **Oil spills**, especially in the Niger Delta region, have had a catastrophic impact on the regional flora and fauna. Other environmental problems include deforestation or soil pollution from mining.

- **Crime:** Nigeria has some influential syndicates of **organised crime**. These specialise in drug trafficking, prostitution and fraud.

- **Human rights violations and gender imbalance:** Despite laws prohibiting child marriages and genital mutilation, girls in particular are often subject to human rights violations. A climate of human rights violations is also furthered by regular police brutality and political corruption.

- **Emigration/Nigeria's "brain drain":** Due to dissatisfaction with the political and economic climate in the country, many highly-skilled Nigerians leave the country (especially to go to the USA).

- **Nigeria's active role in promoting pan-African politics:** Nigeria takes a strong stance for African unity and against White minority governments. The country was one of the most outspoken critics of South Africa's apartheid regime, for example. It has also been central in suggesting a pan-African currency, the Eco.

- **Nigerian culture:** Because of its various ethnic groups, Nigeria has a rich cultural heritage. Besides that, Arabic and Western European influences have further added to the mix. In addition to its thriving **visual arts** and **music** sectors, Nigeria has a particularly prolific **literary** (Wole Soyinka, Nobel prize winner in 1986; Chinua Achebe; Flora Nwapa; Chimamanda Ngozi Adichie; Helon Habila) **and cinematic scene** ("**Nollywood**", the third-biggest film industry in the world).

Shakespeare and his time

date	1550								1620

date: 1550 ... 1620

historical background:
1558: Elizabeth I becomes queen at the age of 25

1603: Elizabeth I dies, James VI of Scotland becomes James I of England

Shakespeare's private life:
1564: William Shakespeare is born in Stratford-upon-Avon

1582: Shakespeare marries Anne Hathaway
1583: birth of daughter Susanna
1585: birth of twins Hamnet and Judith

1596: Shakespeare's son Hamnet dies

1616: Shakespeare dies

Shakespeare's professional life:
late 1580s: Shakespeare comes to London as writer, actor and part-owner of playing company ("Lord Chamberlain's Men")

1599: Globe Theatre built on the south bank of the Thames

1603: Shakespeare's theatre company wins a royal patent ("The King's Men")

1613: retirement to Stratford-upon-Avon

1623: The First Folio, a collection of Shakespeare's plays is published

1589 – 1613: Shakespeare's most productive years as a playwright

Shakespeare's works (examples):
early 1590s: earliest plays (e. g. Henry VI, Richard III, The Taming of the Shrew)
mid 1590s: most acclaimed comedies (e. g. A Midsummer Night's Dream, Much Ado about Nothing)
late 1590s: among some histories, Romeo and Juliet

early 17th century: famous tragedies (e. g. Hamlet, Othello, Macbeth, King Lear)

around 1610: Shakespeare's late works, many of which are difficult to categorise (e. g. The Tempest)

sonnets throughout his career

1 Biography and historical background

1.1 Historical overview

- On the one hand, the "**Elizabethan Age**" is often described as an era of peacefulness and prosperity, a "**Golden Age**" in which the arts, theatre, science and exploration flourished.

- On the other hand, there was also uncertainty:
  - After years of **religious controversy**, Elizabeth I had to keep the peace between Catholics and Protestants.
  - Elizabeth I faced **assassination plots** that tried to replace her with her Catholic cousin, Mary, Queen of Scots.
  - England was attacked by the **Spanish Armada** (1588) and despite England's victory, peace was only made years later.
  - As Elizabeth was unmarried, it was clear that she would **die without an heir**.

- Shakespeare never wrote directly about the political problems and events of his time. However, in his plays, he subtly alludes to the current political situation.

  Examples

  - *Hamlet:* power struggle which leads to the invasion by a king from a neighbouring country
  - *Julius Caesar:* the dangers of civil war after a leader's death

- 1603: After Queen Elizabeth's death, James VI of Scotland became **King James I** of England, ruling both Scotland and England.
  - He made **peace with Spain**.
  - This made it easier for the English to travel the seas and explore the New World. In 1607, the **first colony in Virginia** was called Jamestown in James's honour.
  - The **arts continued to flourish** and, as James liked the theatre, he adopted Shakespeare's company (then called "**The King's Men**").

  Example

  Macbeth: set in James I's native Scotland and depicting his ancestors in a positive way; dealing with witchcraft and supernatural powers, in which James I was very interested

1.2 The Elizabethan worldview

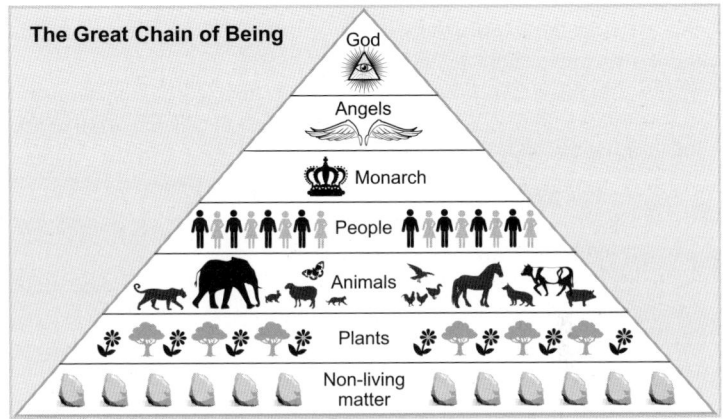

- In the Elizabethan era, people saw **the universe as hierarchically structured**: everything and everyone had a place where they belonged. This order is called the "**Great Chain of Being**".

- The concept originated with Plato and Aristotle and was very influential throughout the Middle Ages up to Shakespeare's time.

- This concept supports the monarchy, because it gives the king or queen (as God's representative on earth) the **divine right to rule**, and any kind of disobedience is a sin.

- It also **stabilises the existing order of society**: whatever your status might be, a noble, a farmer or a beggar, this is the place you were given by God.

- The concept can also be transferred to the family, in which a **patriarchal structure** is seen as the equivalent of an orderly state.

- **Order** (and **disorder**) are important **elements in Shakespeare's plays**: on the one hand, upsetting the natural order can lead to chaos and destruction, while on the other, Shakespeare also plays with the concept and introduces elements of disorder and rebellion – when women speak up against men, for instance.

Examples

- *Macbeth:* When Macbeth illegitimately captures the throne by killing the righteous king, the whole of the natural order is upset and even the horses in the stable go mad.
- *Much Ado about Nothing:* Beatrice, as an unusually outspoken and witty woman, seems almost uncontrollable. Yet, at the end of the play, she does marry Benedick and therefore adapts to the "natural order of things".

1.3 Life and inspirations

- Shakespeare grew up in quite a **wealthy family**.
- He probably went to the local grammar school in Stratford, where he also learnt **Latin and Greek**.
- To establish himself as an actor and playwright, Shakespeare divided his time between **London** and Stratford.
- Shakespeare **used all kinds of sources**: he borrowed from historical portrayals as well as from older tales or plays. This was common practice at the time. However, he often came up with his own details, characters or plotlines, which makes his plays unique.
- "**authorship debate**": Some scholars argue that Shakespeare's rather humble background does not fit the great variety of specialised subjects he deals with in his works. However, doubts about Shakespeare's authorship are a minority opinion today.

1.4 Theatre in Shakespeare's time

- At the beginning of Elizabeth I's reign, most acting companies were **travelling companies**. The **first fixed theatre building** was built in London in **1576** and was simply called "The Theatre".
- Acting companies usually had a **noble patron** who gave his or her name to the company.
- Actors could become rich and famous, but their **reputation** was not too good.

- **Women** were **not allowed on stage**, so boys whose voices had not yet broken often played female roles ("cross-dressing").
- In 1599, Shakespeare's company built their own theatre. Some facts about the "**Globe Theatre**":
  - location: on the **south bank of the Thames**
  - **open-air amphitheatre**
  - "**apron stage**": surrounded by the audience on three sides
  - up to **3,000 spectators**: "**groundlings**" (**pit** in front of the stage), wealthier visitors (covered three-tiered **galleries**)
  - performances only **during daytime**
  - very **few props**

2 Works

Shakespeare is believed to be the author (or co-author) of **39 plays** and **154 sonnets**. His dramas are usually categorised into **comedies, tragedies and histories**, but these categories are not always clear-cut.

2.1 Comedies

Shakespeare's comedy is **different from modern comedy**. Although there may be funny moments, a Shakespearean comedy can involve dramatic storylines. A simple definition of a Shakespearean comedy might be that it has a **happy ending, often involving a marriage**.

Some further typical elements of Shakespeare's comedies are:
- a struggle of young lovers to overcome problems
- elements of separation and reunion
- mistaken identities, often involving disguise
- clever servants
- family tensions that are usually resolved in the end
- complex, interwoven plotlines
- frequent use of puns and other styles of comedy

Examples

- *The Taming of the Shrew* (~1591): Petruchio manages to "tame" the shrew, Katherina, who becomes an obedient wife in the end.
- *A Midsummer Night's Dream* (~1595): Four young Athenian lovers (Hermia, Lysander, Demetrius and Helena) become entangled in the manipulations of the fairy king (Oberon) and queen (Titania) and their servant, Puck.
- *Much Ado about Nothing* (~1598): Two couples finally end up together after Claudio and Hero have been broken up as a result of intrigue while Beatrice and Benedick are at first averse to marriage and only reluctantly admit to being in love.

2.2 Tragedies

Tragedies may include some comic scenes ("**comic relief**"), but generally have serious plots with an ending that shows the death of many of the main characters.

- There is not a clear-cut distinction between tragedies and other genres, for instance histories or so-called "romances" or "tragicomic plays".
- Tragedies can be grouped into two subcategories: **tragedies of fate** and **tragedies of character**. Shakespeare is mainly credited for writing very differentiated and psychologically complex tragedies of character.
  - **tragedy of fate:** There is a sense of doom and the tragic ending seems inevitable or inescapable.

    Example

    Romeo and Juliet (~1597): Romeo and Juliet, whose two families are enemies, fall in love. However, they are "star-crossed lovers", i. e. their love is ill-fated. The play ends with both their suicides.

  - **tragedy of character:** The protagonist, or one of the protagonists, has a character flaw which leads to their downfall despite their noble nature.

Examples

- *Hamlet* (~ 1601): Hamlet, Prince of Denmark, is called upon by the ghost of his dead father to revenge him. However, Hamlet hesitates to execute revenge on his uncle, who has married his mother.
- *Othello* (~ 1603): Against the social conventions of his time, the dark-skinned general of the Venetian army, Othello, has married Desdemona. His subordinate, Iago, manages to arouse Othello's jealousy so much that he ends up killing Desdemona.
- *King Lear* (~ 1605): The elderly King Lear wants to divide his kingdom among his three daughters. Due to his pride, he expels his youngest daughter, Cordelia, who refuses to flatter her father falsely, in contrast to her sisters, Goneril and Regan.
- *Macbeth* (~ 1606): Incited to murderous ambition by three witches and by his wife, Lady Macbeth, Macbeth kills the Scottish king Duncan and usurps his throne.

2.3 Histories

- Shakespeare's histories focus on English monarchs.
- They indirectly support the justice and peacefulness of Queen Elizabeth's reign and show the dangers of civil war.

2.4 Sonnets

- Besides his plays, **Shakespeare wrote 154 sonnets**, which were published in 1609.
- Typical themes of the sonnets are love, jealousy, infidelity, beauty, the passage of time and mortality.
- The first 126 sonnets are **addressed to a young man** and the last 28 addressed to a woman – a mysterious '**Dark Lady**' (the sonnets addressed to the "Dark Lady" are especially innovative as they sarcastically defy the adoration found in traditional sonnets).
- Shakespeare's sonnets have some distinctive features:
  - **14 lines**

- written in **iambic pentameter**: five metrical feet in one line (normally ten syllables), rhythm: "unstressed, stressed"
- **three quatrains** (a set of four lines) and a **rhyming couplet** (a set of two lines) at the end
- rhyme scheme: **abab cdcd efef** (three quatrains) **gg** (rhyming couplet)
- the rhyming couplet often introduces a **surprising new idea** after the three quatrains
- Shakespeare liked to experiment with the sonnet form.

3   Language

- Shakespeare contributed about **1,700 new words** to the English language (by either writing down words that had only been used orally until then or by creatively inventing completely new words). Some of these Shakespeare **neologisms** are still part of everyday English, while others are not.

Example

adjective "**gloomy**" derived from "gloom"

- Furthermore, many **phrases** that are now part of everyday English were first written down by Shakespeare.

Examples

- "method in the madness" *(Hamlet)*
- "wear your heart on your sleeve" *(Othello)*

- In early modern English, there was a distinction between the use of "**thou**", "**thee**", "**thy**" and "**thine**" on the one hand and "**you**" and "**your**" on the other. Whereas "thou" would be used to address personal friends or social inferiors, "you" was the polite form used for addressing superiors or to express courtesy.

- **verse vs. prose:** Nobles would speak in **verse**, servants would speak in **prose**. The use of prose can also be a means of expressing a character's moral corruptness or high emotionality, whereas a person with a low status speaking in verse would show their moral integrity.

> **Example**
>
> Othello normally speaks in verse. However, in his anger and jealousy, he switches to prose.

- Most of Shakespeare's plays are written in **blank verse**, a rhythmic verse form that **does not rhyme**. This verse form is usually written in **iambic pentameter** and imitates the rhythm of natural speech.
- Rhyme is often used in "**rhyming couplets**", which are commonly used to mark the ending of monologues, dialogues, acts or scenes.

> **Example**
>
> final lines of *Romeo and Juliet* (Act V, Scene 2):
> *For never was a story of more woe*
> *Than this of Juliet and her Romeo.*

4 Shakespeare – still relevant today?

Shakespeare is often called the greatest playwright of all time. His works are played in theatres around the world, he is quoted in literature in countless languages and his inventions have been adapted for film, opera, ballet and other forms of art. Some potential **reasons for his ongoing popularity** might be:

- His themes are **psychologically deep** and of timeless relevance.
- Shakespeare took **different philosophical trends and worldviews** into account, e. g. religious faith vs. science, the worldviews of the nobility and the lower classes, reason vs. emotion, etc. This is perfect for modern readers, who can easily identify with a world in upheaval.
- Shakespeare's plays very **rarely offer simple answers** and there are **multiple ways to interpret** them.
- His **characters** are **multidimensional** and often contradictory in their deeds and decisions. This makes them interesting and easy to identify with.
- The plays are also **politically open**: while they can be read as a eulogy on the Tudor reign, they also address other political ideas.

- Shakespeare's plays also **question common norms**, give outcasts a voice and tend to blur the boundaries between "normal" and "mad".

- **Gender roles**, for instance, are often ambiguous and progressive for Shakespeare's age. Women tend to be strong characters and at least partially challenge patriarchal society.

Arguments for and against dealing with Shakespeare at school being compulsory

	discussion topic
Arguments for dealing with Shakespeare being compulsory	**Arguments against dealing with Shakespeare being compulsory**
• Shakespeare's plays deal with **universal human themes** and ask important questions that are still relevant for a modern audience (cf. above). • Shakespeare has had a **lasting influence on the English language and culture**, so his works are an important part of a comprehensive study of English. • The **many adaptations in different formats** can make the study of his plays even more interesting and accessible.	• Shakespeare's plays are **outdated**, which makes their language difficult and some attitudes incomprehensible to modern audiences. • A glorification of Shakespeare and a unique focus on his works ignores other equally talented writers and **does not promote diversity**. • Reading Shakespeare's plays at school is artificial because they were **written to be performed**, not studied.
"Shakespeare was not of an age, but for all time" (cf. Ben Jonson's memorial poem, 1623)	**In a modern curriculum it would be outdated to make dealing with Shakespeare compulsory.**

Stichwortverzeichnis

abortion 30, 36, 71 f.
African American experiences
    22 ff., 31, 34 f., 38, 41
African National Congress
    (ANC) 79
AIDS 80
American Dream 34, 35
American War of Independence
    4, 7, 22
apartheid 78 ff., 84
artificial intelligence (AI) 63 f.,
    68
assimilation 16, 33

Bharatiya Janata Party (BJP) 75
Biden, Joseph 25
Black Lives Matter 8, 17, 25, 35
Brexit 5, 6, 8, 10, 13 f., 16, 71 f.
British Empire 3 f., 7 f., 15 ff., 20,
    22, 31, 44, 50, 74 f., 78, 82 ff.
Britishness 15
Bush, George W. 27

Cameron, David 11, 13
"cancel culture" 36
climate change / environmental
    pollution 30, 36, 46, 47 f., 58,
    60, 63, 64, 67, 68, 84
cloning 61 f., 67, 68
Cold War 24, 26, 44
Commonwealth 7 f., 12, 15, 71,
    75, 78 f., 82
Conservative Party 6, 10 f., 13
constitutional monarchy 4, 9
cultural imperialism 8, 41, 49 ff.

death penalty 37 f.
Declaration of Independence 22,
    35
Democratic Party 30, 36
devolution 2, 5 f., 11
dystopia 62, 65 ff.

Elizabethan Age 3, 5, 7, 20,
    85 ff.
environmental pollution / climate
    change 30, 36, 46, 47 f., 58, 60,
    63, 64, 67, 68, 84
European Union (EU) 4 f., 13 f.,
    15, 38, 51, 71

fake news 57 f.
"filter bubbles" 57 f.
first-past-the-post 10, 28
frontier 35, 37

Gaeltacht 69
Gandhi, Mahatma 75
genetic engineering 59 ff., 68
global conciousness 48, 49 ff.
globalisation 43 ff.
Great Depression 23
gun laws 35, 36 f.

homosexual and transgender
    rights 30, 36, 62, 71

immigration 8, 13 f., 15 ff., 27,
    30, 31 ff., 34, 40, 41, 71
impeachment 28, 29
inauguration 25, 28
India 7, 50, 73 ff.
industrialisation 4, 18, 44, 65, 67

Internet 44 f., 50, 53, 56 ff., 66
Ireland 14, 15, 31, 40, 69 ff.
Irish Republican Army (IRA)
    70 f.

Johnson, Boris 11, 13

King, Martin Luther Dr. 24

Labour Party 6, 10 f., 13
Liberal Democrats 6, 10
lingua franca 8, 50 f.

Magna Carta 3
Mandela, Nelson 79
Manifest Destiny 23, 35
May, Theresa 11, 13
media 20, 27, 41, 43, 53 ff.
Megxit 11 f.
monarchy 11 f., 18, 19, 29
multiculturalism 12, 15 ff., 20,
    31 ff., 36, 39 f., 41, 71, 74 ff.,
    77 ff., 81 ff.

Native Americans 22 f., 31, 34,
    35, 41
Nigeria 81 ff.

Obama, Barack 25

parliamentary democracy 9, 70,
    78
pluralism 16, 33
police violence 16 f., 25, 84
print media 53 ff.

racism 8, 11, 15 ff., 31 f., 34, 38
reformation 3, 70
religion 19, 21, 22, 31 f., 35, 36,
    39 f., 70 ff., 74 ff., 78, 82 f.

Republican Party 23, 30, 36

science fiction 68
Scottish National Party (SNP)
    5 f., 10
segregation 23 f., 78 f.
Shakespeare, William 85 ff.
slavery 8, 22 f., 30, 35, 41, 82
social class 10, 12, 13, 17 f., 20,
    34, 67, 75 f.
social media 52, 56 ff., 66
South Africa 77 ff.
"spin doctors" 54
stem cells 61
sustainability 48, 63, 84

terrorism 16 f., 24, 26, 27, 52, 83
Thatcher, Margaret 4, 11, 18
Trump, Donald 25
Truth and Reconciliation
    Commission (TRC) 79 f.

United Kingdom (UK) 1 ff.,
    69 ff.
United Kingdom Independence
    Party (UKIP) 10, 13
United Nations (UN) 4, 8, 24, 26,
    51
United States of America (USA)
    21 ff., 49 ff.
utopia 65, 68

Windrush 15
women's rights 4, 12, 20, 23, 35,
    64, 67, 72, 75 f., 80, 84, 87 f.,
    94
world of work 58